TEES
VALLEY

CURIOSITIES

TEES VALLEY

CURIOSITIES

ROBERT WOODHOUSE

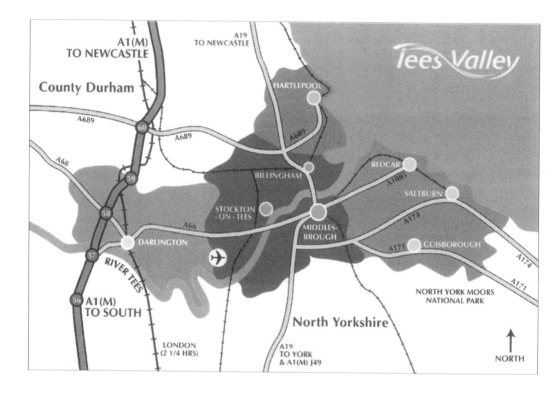

First published 2009

Reprinted 2010

The History Press
The Mill, Brimscombe Port
Stroud, Gloucestershire, GL5 2QG
www.thehistorypress.co.uk

British Library Cataloguing in Publication Data.
A catalogue record for this book is available from the British Library.

ISBN 978 0 7509 5077 0

Typesetting and origination by The History Press
Printed in Great Britain

Contents

Acknowledgements

Having spent most of my life residing on one or other side of the River Tees, I would claim to have a fairly detailed knowledge of the constituent areas of the Tees Valley, but preparing a body of work of this nature has inevitably meant calling on the detailed knowledge of many other local people and organisations.

A considerable amount of information has been gathered from local history departments at Darlington, Hartlepool and Loftus libraries as well as tourist information centres at Saltburn, Stockton and Hartlepool. Other material has been provided by Ann Gladwin, Countryside Officer for Middlesbrough Council; Peter Rowe, from Tees Archaeology, and members of the Tees Valley Wildlife Trust. I am indebted to all these agencies for their diligence and expertise in locating and supplying information.

Specific information on different locations has been provided by Stuart Ramsdale (Redcar and Cleveland area), Alan Suddes (Darlington), Geoff Braddy and Peter McTiernan (Middlesbrough), and Tony Lynn (Saltburn district). I offer my grateful thanks to all of these people for their support and assistance.

The warmth and friendliness of local people was clearly evident when offering support in finding specific locations and, on a practical level, Sandra Mylan has provided invaluable secretarial support.

Introduction

In recent years there have been several changes in local government administration resulting in alteration to boundaries. As a Yorkshireman by birth and upbringing I regret the disappearance of traditional county boundaries and view the latest arrangement of areas as 'The Tees Valley' with a little consternation. This grouping of very diverse localities represents something of a curiosity in itself!

Contrasts abound in the Tees Valley area, with industrial landmarks ranging from the dramatic outlines of the Transporter and Newport Bridges to the pyramid-like Kiltonthorpe Tip in East Cleveland, while the beacon tower on Eston Nab gave warning of impending invasion, and across the Tees estuary at Hartlepool medieval town walls offered protection to citizens on the Headland.

Hartlepool's monkey legend has led to any number of local sporting links, but less well known is the story behind the stag on premises in Middlesbrough's Linthorpe Road. The remains of a primeval forest on the foreshore at Hartlepool are only visible at low tide, but a rare, black poplar tree dominates the roadside setting on Green Lane in Middlesbrough.

A whole assortment of unusual buildings are dotted around the Tees Valley. They range from the tiny dimensions of Yarm Castle to the decorative features of Cliff House, while an air of mystery surrounds Winky's Castle at Marske and Saltburn's old mortuary. Other properties display curious features such as the figurehead on the White Hart Inn in Hart village and the wonderfully decorative doors in former bank premises in Middlesbrough's Albert Road.

Tees Valley may be a recent administrative arrangement, but it has drawn together a truly varied collection of curiosities.

Visiting the Curiosities

The curiosities covered in this book are to be found in a whole range of locations. Several are landmarks and these are probably best viewed from a distance (especially when close inspection may involve a demanding ascent). A number are privately owned (as domestic or business premises) and must be viewed from the roadside, while some are subject to normal opening times.

The curiosities can be visited either singly or in groups. A few are in fairly remote countryside and can only be reached on foot, but the large majority are accessible by public transport.

Due care and attention should be exercised in terms of traffic on public roads and uneven ground or severe gradients.

one

Redcar and
Cleveland

WINKIE'S CASTLE

HIDDEN SECRETS OF A CRUCK-BUILT COTTAGE

Access

Winkie's Castle is located on the east side of Marske High Street (A1085), close to the central roundabout. Opening times should be checked through Redcar, Saltburn or Guisborough Tourist Information Centres.

The busy coastal township of Marske has its origins in the Anglo-Saxon period and though there are few records from those early days it is possible to pick out a number of fascinating properties along the High Street.

Marske's oldest house is located at 162 High Street. Known locally as 'Winkie's Castle', it dates back to about 1500 AD and is a fine example of a 'cruck house', where upright curving oak timbers were secured at the top. Space between the crucks was usually filled with wattle and daub while a thatched roof rested on the rafters.

Timber for this intriguing house probably came from ships that ran aground locally or possibly from the thirteenth-century Fauconberg Castle, which stood in the field on the south side of the railway station.

Cruck houses could easily be extended by adding pairs of crucks at each end and fastening them to the others by the ridge pole and purlins. The enlarged 'long houses' could accommodate the family, cattle, horses, hens and farm equipment.

Winkie's Castle, No. 162 High Street, Marske-by-the-Sea.

An interesting feature of many of these cottages was the witch post – a vertical timber at the entrance of the living room which not only held up the hearth beam but also warded off evil spirits. The inglenook behind the witch post was not only a warm place to sit but also a 'safe' refuge and a stone bench or settle was usually placed here.

During the late twentieth century, Jack Anderson assembled a collection of local history items in Winkie's Castle, and since his death this intriguing property has been re-opened as a folk museum.

STOUPS

MODERN REMINDERS OF AN OLD MOORLAND ROUTE

A line of six upright stones on the north side of the Guisborough to Whitby (A171) Moor Road near Birk Brow serve as a reminder of the difficulties of overland travel in the days before modern road systems.

Access

The stoups are clearly visible alongside the A171 road a few hundred yards east of the car park close to the summit of Birk Brow. (A footpath runs alongside the A171 on the south side).

The Six Stoups alongside the A171 Moor Road.

For several hundred years a set of stone posts marked a safe route across a boggy stretch of moorland, but in more recent times they suffered damage from modern traffic and highway maintenance work. During February 2005, members of the Rotary Club of Guisborough and Great Ayton co-operated with Redcar and Cleveland Council to replace the set of six roadside stoups and their efforts were recognised at the Rotary Clubs' regional conference at Leeds in February 2006.

They received the regional award for the best environmental project organised by a Rotary Club by involving the local community in the restoration of a piece of local heritage.

Stoups – looking east along the A171.

REDCAR'S DISH MIRROR

A LITTLE-KNOWN EARLY-WARNING DEFENCE SYSTEM

In recent years the early-warning defence systems at Fylingdales (south of Whitby) and Menwith Hill (near Harrogate) have made regular headlines, but these space-age installations represent only the latest attempt to defend England's eastern seaboard.

During the late fourth century AD, Roman forces constructed a line of signal stations along the Yorkshire coast at locations such as Huntcliff, Goldsborough and Scarborough to give warning of raiding parties, but by the early twentieth century the threat of attack came from the skies, as well as the sea.

German warships had bombarded Scarborough, Whitby and Hartlepool in December 1914, but by 1916 it was airships that posed a novel and sinister threat. From their base at Nordholtz, Zeppelins targeted industrial sites on Teesside and in particular Skinningrove Iron Works, where secret work was being carried out.

The first line of defence against night attacks was by intercepting radio messages at stations at locations such as Stockton, and airships were also spotted from the ground by the forerunners of the Royal Observer Corps. The time gap between the two methods of detection was filled by concrete acoustic mirrors.

Zeppelins made a total of fifteen raids on the north-east coast between April 1915 and November 1917, and the sound of these enemy airships was reflected off the concave 'mirror' surface into a trumpet mounted on a steel column. From there the sound was transferred to a stethoscope which allowed a 'listener' to determine the direction of an approaching aircraft.

Sound detection technology was replaced by 'reflective detection finding' – later known as radar by the early 1940s – but these concrete acoustic mirrors continued in use until 1944.

A dish mirror at Wheatlands Farm, Redcar, faced north east to guard the Tees estuary. Another was sited at Boulby Cliff, close to an earlier Armada beacon site, to give warning to the nearby Skinningrove ironworks, and a third Yorkshire mirror in the form of a cruder slab device is located at Kilnsea near Spurn Head.

Access
The dish mirror stands beside the roadside verge at Wheatlands Farm, close to the southern end of Redcar Lane (B1269).

Above: *Plaque commemorating the history of the mirror.* Below: *The dish mirror at Wheatlands Farm, Redcar.*

ST ANDREW'S, UPLEATHAM

ONE OF THE COUNTRY'S SMALLEST CHURCHES

The tiny church of St Andrew at Upleatham has often been described as the smallest church in England. Set in rolling countryside on the north side of Skelton Beck, it was at the heart of the original community, but

Access

St Andrew's Church is on the south side of the B1268 to the south east of Upleatham Village.

St Andrew's Church, Upleatham.

in fact the present building represents only a small part of an earlier Norman church.

Much of the original church was demolished in 1836 when a replacement church was constructed further up the hillside. The tower, at best, dates from 1684, but the east wall was completed during the nineteenth century in order to fashion a mortuary chapel from part of the twelfth-century nave.

Excavations during the early 1970s revealed that the present building, measuring 18ft (5.5m) long by 15ft (4.5m) wide, was originally almost twice as large. The discovery of stone fragments from a ninth-century cross point to a pre-Conquest place of worship on the site, and other items of stonework that have been unearthed include a stone effigy of a fourteenth-century knight and an eleventh-century child's grave slab.

The Norman font was transferred to the later church (which has also closed in recent years).

WARSETT HILL, NEAR BROTTON

A CURIOUS CLIFF-TOP STRUCTURE

Access

The fan house is close to the cliff edge, on the Cleveland Way between Saltburn and Skinningrove.

A strange concrete structure on the cliff top below Warsett Hill probably inspires thoughts of a coastguard station, fog horn or even a remnant of a medieval fortress. In fact, this gaunt relic is a link with the area's recent industrial past, when ironstone mining flourished throughout east Cleveland.

Taking its name from a Belgian inventor, the Guibal fan house was designed in 1862 and this ventilation shaft served the nearby Huntcliff Mine (which operated from 1872 to 1906). A 9m-diameter fan revolved at 49rpm to drive oxygen for men, horses and naked lights into the mine, whilst also drawing out smoke and fumes after the hard rock had been blasted.

Guibal's design of the fan created a more efficient air flow, with a sliding shutter allowing the air flow to be regulated through the chimney. The chimney itself had a special design feature to reduce resistance when delivering air, and the whole operation was powered by a steam engine.

Guibal fan house, below Warsett Hill.

This type of ventilation shaft became popular in Britain during the 1870s, but from 1910 they were replaced by more efficient versions driven by electricity.

MOORSHOLM DOCKS

DOCKS OF A VERY DIFFERENT TYPE

Mention of docks probably conjures up an image of a harbour or quayside, but nothing could be further from the truth in the case of Moorsholm Docks. This pleasant rural community lies close to the Guisborough to Whitby (A171) road, within sight of the strange outline of Freeborough Hill, and the 'docks' in question are no more than a set of roadside stone troughs for watering passing livestock.

Access

Moorsholm Docks are located beside the High Street at the northern end of the village, which is one mile north of Birk Brow (A171) Road.

Moorsholm Docks on the village's High Street.

They probably originate from the late nineteenth century, at a time when the price of a trough was based on the number of gallons of water it would hold. A trough measuring 10ft 8in (3.2m) by 3ft 3in (1m) and 2ft 6in (0.76m) in depth would probably cost £3.

In recent years these sturdy stone basins have been restored and serve as an intriguing reminder of this area's agricultural past.

OUTDOOR PULPIT ON THE FORMER LOFTUS UNITED REFORM CHURCH

A RARE PREACHING POINT

Access

The Loftus United Reform Church (now closed) is located on the corner of the High Street and North Road at Loftus.

Church pulpits are to be found in all sorts of shapes and sizes. They represent an essential element in most services and religious ceremonies, but it is very unusual to find an outdoor pulpit.

Early members of the Congregational Church in Loftus were based at the town's Ebenezer Chapel from 1827, but during the late nineteenth century these premises proved to be inadequate. Fundraising during the early twentieth century led to the opening of a fine, new Congregational Church in 1906.

Located on the corner of the High Street and North Road, this imposing red-brick building has horizontal bands of sandstone around its two sides and tower, but its most intriguing feature is the outdoor pulpit. This strategic vantage point allowed church workers to address members of the public on adjacent pavements and may well have been used by Revd T. Coledge, who began his ministry as a pastor at Loftus in 1907.

The building became part of Loftus United Reform Church in the mid-1980s but closed as a place of worship in 2004. Developers subsequently submitted a scheme to convert the church into flats and a condition of the agreement was that the pulpit must be preserved for future generations.

The outdoor pulpit of Loftus United Reform Church.

PADDY WADDELL'S RAILWAY

THE RAILWAY THAT NEVER SAW A LOCOMOTIVE

Access

Embankments
and cuttings
mark the
route of the
railway from
Moorsholm
across open
moorland
towards
Glaisdale.

North-east England makes a strong claim to being the birthplace of the nation's railway network. Originating first as tramways linking coal mines with major river systems such as the Tyne, Wear and, later, the Tees, railways also played a vital role in exploiting deposits of ironstone in North Yorkshire. Cuttings, embankments and bridges offer clues to the mineral lines that linked up with major rail routes.

The most curious of all these lines was the Cleveland Mineral Extension Railway, which is better known as Paddy Waddell's Railway. It had a protracted and eventful life span, but never actually opened for business.

The promoter of the line was Joseph Dodds from Winston, near Barnard Castle, and subscribers to his scheme included Carl Bolckow and a local landowner, Lord Downe. The scheme was intended to transport ironstone from mines in the East Cleveland area around Skelton and Brotton across the North York Moors for about 10 miles to ironworks at Glaisdale in the Esk Valley.

Early attempts to win parliamentary approval were thwarted by promoters of a line between Whitby and Loftus, and although the Glaisdale ironworks were operational from 1866, it was the summer of 1873 before the bill was given royal assent.

Joseph Dodds took centre stage at a ceremonial turf cutting in the outlying village of Moorsholm, and the line's engineer was John Waddell, whose earlier projects included London's Putney Bridge, the Mersey Rail Tunnel and the Whitby, Loftus and Whitby-Scarborough railways. Waddell's nickname, 'Paddy', may have originated from the hordes of Irish navvies who carried out heavy manual work on his engineering projects.

Following the ceremony at Moorsholm, and the completion of a prominent yellow-brick railway hotel in the village, the project ran into severe difficulties. Financial backing for ongoing construction work did not materialise and, as the scheme faltered, revival acts had to be obtained in 1878 and 1881. Phases of activity followed by inaction resulted in a total of seven acts sanctioning building work on the line through to 1896.

Apart from the imposing but incongruous railway hotel at Moorsholm (which was demolished in the mid-1990s), there are several other reminders of this ill-fated project. Cottages close to Glaisdale and Lealholm served as temporary inns for construction workers, and embankments and a cutting on either side of the A171 road, west of Scaling Dam, mark the line of the route.

The Station Hotel, Moorsholm (demolished in the mid-1990s).

A dramatic decline in countrywide railway building and the closure of the ironworks at Glaisdale, followed by long-term depression in the iron trade during the 1880s, meant that the Cleveland Mineral Extension Railway – better known as 'Paddy Waddell's Railway' – was never completed. Perhaps the most surprising aspect is that promoters and interested parties persisted for quite so long with a scheme that now seems to have been impossible from the outset.

ALBERT MEMORIAL

CLASSICAL TEMPLE IN A NATURAL SETTING

Access

The Albert Memorial is set in woodland below Glenside at Saltburn.

The spreading greenery of Saltburn's Valley Gardens is an unlikely location for a classical-style temple. Set at the top of a long flight of stone steps, high above Skelton Beck, it has a porch with two pairs of Corinthian columns supporting a pedimented panel and curved rear wall (that was added later).

This curious structure was originally the entrance portico to Barnard Castle railway station, but it was transported to the developing Victorian resort of Saltburn-by-the-Sea by Henry Pease, and repositioned in the Valley Gardens as a memorial to Prince Albert, Queen Victoria's consort, who died in 1861.

SALTBURN MORTUARY

SOBERING REMINDER OF THE NORTH SEA'S VICTIMS

Access

The mortuary building is set alongside Saltburn Road (below Cat Nab), close to the Ship Inn.

Saltburn-by-the-Sea gained widespread fame as a high-class Victorian resort with a whole range of attractions, including croquet lawns and band concerts as well as dramatic sea views. Yet the town had much humbler origins in the shape of a shoreline hamlet close to Cat Nab.

The Albert Memorial in Saltburn's Valley Gardens.

Few of the early buildings survive apart from the row of properties that include the Ship Inn, but another row, at the foot of Cat Nab, included the Nimrod Inn where an old mortuary building now stands. Minutes of meetings of the local boards for Brotton and Saltburn chart the progress of the construction of this curious little structure.

During the period between November 1880 and February 1881, meetings of the two boards indicate that the estimated cost of £80 was to be met 'out of their rates or by means of private subscriptions', and on 5 August 1881 the local board of Brotton authorised building work.

On 3 February 1882 the local board for the District of Brotton agreed that 5s per year should be paid to Mr Temple for taking charge of the mortuary. Later in the year, on 1 September 1882, it was unanimously agreed that the surveyor should 'expend a sum not exceeding £5 in protecting the mortuary by wooden props or other efficient means from the slipping of Cat Nab'. Some six months later, on 2 March 1883, the board accepted a tender from Mr Thomas Dickinson for construction of a concrete wall and drain at the mortuary at a cost of £14 12s.

Down the following decades, many victims were no doubt brought to the mortuary by members of the local lifeboat crew. Saltburn lifeboat station was housed in an adjacent building and, although it closed in 1922 (with the transfer of the motor lifeboat to the Teesmouth station), the mortuary continued in use until the later decades of the twentieth century.

Mortuary building below Cat Nab at Saltburn.

KILTONTHORPE SCHOOL

THE SCHOOL THAT NEVER WAS

Exploitation of ironstone deposits in the late nineteenth century led to the growth of whole new communities in many parts of East Cleveland. In 1875 the Kilton Iron Co. opened a mine midway between Carlin How and Brotton, and, in addition to three rows of thirty houses, the community included a splendid set of school buildings.

Desks, blackboards and books were installed in the schoolroom, but no pupils ever arrived for lessons. A strike among ironstone miners was followed by recession and the building remained unused apart from staging wedding receptions. It had no running water or drainage and, although the adjacent schoolmaster's house became a domestic residence, the schoolroom was only used as a forestry store.

Empty houses in the tiny community remained unoccupied and were eventually demolished, while the school became increasingly overgrown and dilapidated. Kilton mine closed in 1963 and the roofless, red-brick school building with pointed Gothic-style windows was left open to the elements until the mid-1990s, when it was tastefully restored as a private residence.

Access
The former school is privately owned and is located at the southern end of Kiltonthorpe village, between Carlin How and Lingdale.

The former Kiltonthorpe School.

ALL SAINTS', SKELTON-IN-CLEVELAND

A CHURCH WITH AN UNUSUAL TOWER

Access

All Saints'
Church is
located at the
eastern end of
Skelton High
Street.

During the later decades of the nineteenth century, many parts of East Cleveland (between Guisborough and the Yorkshire coast) were transformed by the ironstone boom which saw tiny farming communities growing rapidly in order to house workers at nearby mines.

At Skelton, east of Guisborough, several new settlements (New Skelton, North Skelton and Skelton Green) were built away from the original heart of the village. An impressive new church, All Saints', was completed at the east end of the High Street in 1884.

Representing quite a contrast to the old church close to the castle, it has an unusual south porch tower; instead of being incorporated into the main church building, the tower is separated from the west end by a short linking passage.

TIMM'S COFFEE HOUSE, SKINNINGROVE

Q: WHEN IS A COFFEE HOUSE NOT A COFFEE HOUSE?
A: WHEN IT'S AN INN!

Access

Timm's Coffee
House is
prominent in
The Square at
the centre of
Skinningrove.
(Access via
Loftus Bank
on the A174
from Brotton or
Loftus).

Coffee houses became popular as meeting places to exchange gossip, listen to lectures or draw up business deals. Their heyday in London and across Europe was from around 1650 and it seems that this imposing building in the centre of Skinningrove was given its name after the owner and lord of the manor, A.L. Maynard, returned from Fleet Street in London during the early nineteenth century.

The building originally served as the manor house and its early days as an inn have given rise to unlikely tales of local miners calling in for an early breakfast of rum and coffee before setting off for the morning shift.

Above: *All Saints' Church, Skelton-in-Cleveland.*

Right: *Timm's Coffee House, Skinningrove.*

KILTONTHORPE TIP AND FREEBOROUGH HILL

TWO DISTINCTIVE SUMMITS: ONE MAN-MADE AND THE OTHER ENTIRELY NATURAL

Access

Kiltonthorpe Lane runs in a southerly direction from Brotton and the Brotton Bypass (A174) towards Lingdale and Stanghow.

Travelling southwards from Brotton along Kiltonthorpe Lane, there are two striking landscape features: one was made by man, and the other is completely natural.

A tall, conical mound close to the village of Kiltonthorpe is one of the few remaining shale heaps from East Cleveland's nineteenth-century ironstone boom. Mining operations began in Kilton in 1874 and, after a period of closure between 1875 and 1897, it continued in use until 1963. Over the years, a grey and reddish brown heap was built up during operations below the surface, and the tip's shape and colouring provide a striking contrast with the greenery of surrounding land.

Away to the south, beyond the village of Moorsholm, and close to the Moors Road (A171) is the well-known landmark of Freeborough Hill. Its rounded outlines rise 150ft above nearby fields and moorland to a peak of 821ft above sea level. It was once thought to be a tumulus (burial mound) and has inspired no end of folk tales, but experts have concluded that this strange rounded eminence is, in fact, entirely natural. In geological terms it is an outlying section of the Kelloway Rock outcrop on nearby Moorsholm Moor and is, in many respects, similar to the equally celebrated local landmark, Roseberry Topping.

TURNER ESTATES AT KIRKLEATHAM

ORNAMENTAL FEATURES – SOME IN MILITARY MODE

The village of Kirkleatham, near Redcar, is well known for Sir William Turner's splendid set of hospital buildings. Dating from 1676, they comprise a central chapel with adjoining almshouses enclosing a wide courtyard.

Kiltonthorpe Tip (left) and Freeborough Hill (right).

Access

Aspects of the former Turner estates at Kirkleatham are sandwiched between the A1042 Kirkleatham Lane and A174 Kirkleatham bypass on the southern edge of Redcar.

Later members of the Turner family added a Free School building in 1708 (now known as Kirkleatham Old Hall Museum) as well as the mausoleum attached to the church (in 1740) and a range of Gothic-style pavilions, dovecotes and ice houses. Many of these features have disappeared in recent years, including the original hall (dating from the 1660s and demolished in 1956), but surviving structures include a number of bastions (rounded turrets) which represent a set of fanciful 'defences' around the perimeter of Kirkleatham Hall gardens. During the nineteenth century, fear of invasion by seaborne forces spread along England's eastern coastline and plans were prepared to man these garden features as part of measures to repel enemy forces.

Central chapel at Sir William Turner's Almshouses, Kirkleatham.

Battlemented turret close to the main entrance to Sir William Turner's Almshouses.

Bastion on the Turner estate, opposite St Cuthbert's Church, Kirkleatham.

SALTBURN BEACH SLIPWAYS

SEASIDE SLIPWAY WITH A RAILWAY BACKGROUND

Access

The slipways link the lower promenade with the beach close to Saltburn Pier.

Each year thousands of visitors make their way from Saltburn's lower promenade to the beach down stone slipways, but how many people appreciate the origins of these durable blocks?

Close inspection of these large stones reveals tell-tale signs that they originally served as railway sleepers dating from about 1865. Recent research has shown that they were not used on the Stockton and Darlington line, but supported rails on wagonways from collieries in County Durham.

Transported to Saltburn by rail, the stone blocks were moved from the station goods yard down Saltburn Bank, by horse and wagon, to the promenade where they were cut to size and positioned using a tripod. Recent work to install new sewers uncovered a dump composed of surplus stones while the high quality of the sandstone blocks ensures that the distinctive features of former railway sleepers remain clearly visible.

Saltburn's slipways with former railway sleepers.

CLIFF HOUSE

WHIMSICAL TOUCHES TO A VICTORIAN HOLIDAY RETREAT

An array of battlements, turrets and chimneys add a whimsical touch to the prominent building at the seaward end of Cliff Terrace in Marske. Cliff House was built in the mid-1840s as a summer residence for Joseph Pease and his family.

An unofficial regulation ruled that during visits by the Pease family, local folk kept to the Saltburn side of Cliff House. When north-east breezes proved to be rather too bracing, residents at Cliff House could resort to the deep trench that ran behind the boundary wall or rest among ferns and vines in the long conservatory.

During the 1930s, the property was bought by the Holiday Fellowship of the Methodist Church, and following closure in 1974, it was taken over by the Church Army Housing Association. Refurbishment delayed the re-opening until 1981 when it became retirement apartments.

Access

Cliff House occupies a cliff-top position at the seaward end of Cliff Terrace at Marske.

Cliff House overlooking the beach at Marske.

ESTON BEACON

MONUMENT WITHIN A HILL-TOP ENCAMPMENT

Access

Eston Beacon
is accessible
from Eston
(via the B1380
Eston Road and
Southgate) or
via footpaths
close to Cross
Keys Inn (on
the A171
Middlesbrough
Road).

The simple stone monument on Eston Nab has a plaque which explains that it replaced an earlier beacon tower dating from about 1800. Built by Thomas Jackson of Lackenby, the original tower served as a look-out post during the threat of invasion by Napoleon Bonaparte's forces and was used as such throughout the Second World War.

For a few post-war years, the tower remained in use as a house but, when it was unoccupied, a spate of vandalism resulted in demolition. The replacement monument is surrounded by the ditch and earthworks of a Bronze-Age encampment and this hill-top location makes a superb vantage point for taking views across large tracts of the lower Tees Valley.

*Eston Beacon on Eston Nab,
above Lackenby Bank.*

CLEVELAND WAY IRONSTONE SCULPTURES

STRIKING METALWORK IN A DRAMATIC SETTING

A dramatic cliff-top setting between Saltburn and Skinningrove is the location for a fascinating set of metal sculptures. Manufactured at nearby British Steel Skinningrove, they are the work of Richard Farrington and reflect aspects of Skelton and Brotton parish.

The most striking piece of work is the circle which measures 7 ft in diameter. From its inner rim hang ten sculpted images, ranging from animals such as a horse (Cleveland Bay) and cat to a starfish and nautilus/belemnite (denoting fossils).

Other smaller, solid sculpted pieces represent a trawl door (with large fish) and an upright marker post with four attached metal objects relating to the sky, air, sea and earth. (The sculptures represent one of the projects organised by Tees Valley Arts – formerly Cleveland Arts.)

Access

The sculptures are positioned alongside the Cleveland Way near Warsett Hill and can be reached from Saltburn, Skinningrove or Brotton (via Ings Lane).

Ironstone sculpture on the Cleveland Way, near Warsett Hill.

TOWER AND STEEPLE OF ST GERMAIN'S CHURCH

LANDMARK SURVIVOR ON AN ANCIENT CHURCH SITE

Access

The tower
and steeple of
St Germain's
Church is set
within the
churchyard
at the eastern
end of St
Germain's Lane
at Markse.

Set among gravestones of a spreading churchyard, the tower and steeple of St Germain's Church at Marske continues to withstand a battering from the elements.

Tower and steeple of St Germain's Church, Marske.

The site has been a place of worship for around 1,200 years and the tower offers clues to earlier phases of its history. A lower set of lines show the roof level of the early church that was demolished in 1821, while the upper set mark the line of the rebuilt church which included a small gallery at the rear.

Until 1861, St Germain's Church served Marske, Redcar and properties toward Saltburn, but construction of St Mark's in the centre of Marske in 1867 saw the headland church fall into disrepair. During the 1950s the main body of the church was demolished, leaving the tower and steeple as a navigational landmark for local fishermen.

A recent programme of refurbishment opened it up for use as a tiny chapel and links with the nearby burial of James Cook's father and members of the local smuggling fraternity, in the late 1700s, only add to the charm of this memorable structure.

SALTBURN CLIFF LIFT

WATER-BORNE LINK BETWEEN CLIFF TOP AND PROMENADE

Following the arrival of the railway in 1861, Saltburn was developed as a select Victorian resort with an impressive array of seaside attractions. The most prominent feature of this development was the pier and, between 1870 and 1883, holidaymakers were lowered a hair-raising 150ft in a cage from town-based hotels on the cliff top to beach level by means of a vertical hoist.

This flimsy structure continued in use until a damning report led to its rapid closure and demolition. A rather less alarming system was constructed in the form of an inclined tramway following the opening of two similar structures at Scarborough.

Apart from the replacement of the main winding wheel in 1998 and installation of a modern hydraulic braking system, the lift has changed little since its original opening. Following conversion of Scarborough's cliff lift to electricity, Saltburn's splendid structure is now probably the world's oldest surviving water-balanced cliff lift.

Access
The cliff lift descends from the marine parade to the lower promenade opposite Saltburn Pier.

It carries in excess of 100,000 passengers each summer season, but there are still some visitors who are unwilling to commit themselves to the gentle ascent/descent which lasts some fifty-five seconds.

Saltburn's cliff lift.

two

Stockton-
on-Tees

ROADSIDE HORSE TROUGH

A REFRESHING STOP FOR BEASTS OF BURDEN

Access

The trough is located on the east side of Hartburn Bank below the junction with Hartburn Avenue and Hartburn Lane.

A curious semi-circular ring of stonework on the side of Hartburn Bank (on the west side of Stockton-on-Tees) is an unlikely survivor from an earlier era when horse-drawn transport was the order of the day.

Although the lower section of the structure is now covered by the raised pavement, it is possible to recognise a trough for watering horses as they negotiated the steep gradient.

A plaque reads: 'Erected by Charles Arthur Head Hartburn Hall 1886'. (Hartburn Hall stood on land between Darlington Road and Harlsey Road on the west side of Hartburn. The North and South Lodges are still standing, but the hall was demolished around 1930 and the site was developed with housing.)

The trough on Hartburn Bank.

Plaque on Hartburn Bank.

STOCKTON CASTLE STONEWORK

LOST LINKS WITH A BISHOP'S PALACE

Until the mid-seventeenth century, Stockton Castle covered a large site in central Stockton, but following demolition, the stonework was re-used in many parts of the township. Amounts of stone were used in the lower levels of buildings in Finkle Street and adjacent parts of the High Street, while other quantities have been identified in Ropner Park and Hartburn Lane.

Another identifiable item of castle stonework, the 'Lion Stone', was found in a farmyard at Hartburn before being moved to Elton, where it was used to mark the burial place of a famous race horse, Othello. From here, it was taken into the vestibule of the old Borough Hall, but when this High Street building was itself demolished, the 'Lion Stone' disappeared among the debris. In 1952, it was re-discovered in a heap of rubble at the north end of the lake in Ropner Park and during recent years it has been stored in museum premises in central Stockton.

Access

No. 95 Hartburn Village is privately owned, but the frontage is visible from the public road.

No. 95 Hartburn Village.

No. 95 Hartburn Village is built of regular blocks of yellow Triassic sandstone and has architectural features which suggest that it most probably originated from Stockton Castle.

Access

Plaques and stonework are visible from the public road at the eastern end of Hartburn Village (in front of the red-brick Anglican Church building).

FLAX MAKING AND THE WASHINGTON FAMILY – THE HARTBURN LINKS

A PAIR OF INTRIGUING PLAQUES

Stonework outside the red-brick church building in Hartburn Village provides fascinating insights into earlier aspects of the area's history.

A plaque at the lower level highlights the link with the Wessyngton (Washington) family and the Unites States of America's founding President, George Washington. Unveiled in 1983, the plaque celebrates

Monumental stone in Hartburn Village.

Left and below: *Plaques on the stones in Hartburn Village.*

the re-enactment by local dignitaries of the Hertburne family's move to Washington some 800 years earlier.

The higher plaque is embedded in a large boulder that was found beside the nearby beck. It was used to beat flax at a time in the mid-nineteenth century when large numbers of local women were involved in linen making, and an inscription explains that it was positioned on this site in June 1897 to mark the sixtieth year of Queen Victoria's reign.

THORNABY GREEN

HISTORIC HEART OF A SPREADING MODERN TOWNSHIP

During the last century and a half Thornaby has spread northwards beside the Tees and, more recently, in a southerly direction across the former airfield site, but there are tantalising glimpses of the town's origins around the green.

Within yards of the busy A1045 (Thornaby Road), the spreading expanse of grass has a series of curious earthworks that offer clues to the township's origins.

The Church of St Peter Ad Vincula (meaning St Peter in chains) is prominent in a central position, and fragments of stonework in the walls suggest links with a pre-Conquest building. In 1129, Peter de Brus, Lord of Skelton, gave the Canons of Guisborough Priory ecclesiastical rights at both Stainton and Thornaby, though it seems that Thornaby was subordinate to Stainton.

This original church was dedicated to St Mary Magdalene and, because it had no parochial rights, Grace Pace, mother of Captain James Cook, was married at Stainton Church in October 1725.

Following the opening of St Paul's Church in 1858, the old village church was used only as a cemetery chapel and during 1907-8 it was closed for a programme of alterations under the direction of the Durham-based architect, Hodgson Fowler. At this point the dedication was changed to St Peter Ad Vincula, and further changes were made during the twentieth century, including the replacement of gas lighting by electricity in 1967.

Access

Thornaby Green is west of the A1045 via Green Lane or Upper Green Lane.

St Peter's Church, Thornaby Green.

The local authority took over the disused churchyard around St Peter's in 1968, and during 1970 the churchyard hedge and gate were removed, while headstones were moved to the east end of the graveyard.

The north side of St Peter's Church has an array of earthworks which probably relate to the site of the original village. While some ridges, mounds and dips may well mark the location of one or more dew ponds and boundaries of properties and adjoining gardens, other earthworks continue to generate debate. Aerial photographs have highlighted a series of circular markings at the centre of this open location and explanations range from a henge or gun battery to windmill.

Twentieth-century housing developments have enclosed the green, leaving only Green Farm, at the northern end, and the range of cottages, including Sundial Cottage (dated 1621), to provide intriguing reminders of an earlier township.

Sundial Cottage at the southern end of Thornaby Green.

TRUE LOVERS' WALK

ROMANCE AND DRAMA ON YARM'S RIVERBANK

Access

True Lovers'
Walk runs from
the upstream
side of Yarm
Bridge along
the riverbank
to the parish
church.

The lane that leads from Yarm High Street to the river bank (on the upstream side) has the intriguing name 'True Lovers' Walk', but there is an amount of uncertainty about its origins. Perhaps the most plausible explanation links the pathway with a carving of male and female figures in the nearby parish church.

From the riverbank there is a fine view of the road bridge which has enjoyed a chequered history of its own. The earliest stone bridge was constructed in about 1400 AD on the orders of Walter Skirlaw, Bishop of Durham, and replaced a timber structure that had spanned the Tees for the previous 200 years.

Bishop Skirlaw's bridge was about half the width of the present one and close inspection of the underside of the arches shows the earlier ribbed vaulting and smooth, later sections linked with the road-widening phase.

During the English Civil War of the early 1640s, the arch on the Durham bank was removed and replaced by a drawbridge. Revd Dr Isaac Basire, Rector of Egglescliffe, was entrusted with the duty of pulling up the drawbridge each night. Until a bridge was completed between Stockton and Thornaby in the 1770s, Yarm Bridge represented the lowest crossing point on the Tees and, on 1 February 1643, Royalist and Parliamentary forces clashed at this important strategic location. (The drawbridge at the northern side of the bridge was replaced in 1785 by the curved arch which is different from the earlier pointed arches).

As trade and traffic increased during the late eighteenth century, the 12ft-wide bridge was proving to be inadequate and plans were prepared to replace it with a single-span iron bridge. Work was completed by September 1805, but a dispute over costs of the new section of roadway on the Yarm side meant that it remained unopened, and during the early hours of 12 January 1806 the new bridge met a dramatic demise. Under the weight of ironwork, the south abutment collapsed and the bridge crashed into the Tees. (Most of the iron was sold as scrap, but in 1908 Mr George Goldie, landlord of the Blue Bell Inn, dragged a girder from the river and had it installed in the ceiling of the inn). An inquiry by a panel of architects blamed the collapse of the bridge on the hollow nature of the south abutment and the decision was made to retain and widen the earlier stone bridge.

Yarm railway viaduct, with the road bridge and St John's Church at Egglescliffe in the distance.

The arch of the bridge on the Yarm side became known as the 'sand arch' and, up until 1936, the Wilson family dredged deposits of sand from here and transported it by barge for use in Stockton.

True Lovers' Walk continues along the river bank to St Mary's Church – the third building on the site. There is no sign of the timber-built Saxon church, and the Norman church was extensively damaged by fire in 1728. Restoration work was completed by 1730, making use of amounts of the stone from the earlier building.

YARM METHODIST CHAPEL

JOHN WESLEY'S FAVOURITE PLACE OF WORSHIP

Numbered among Yarm's collection of fascinating buildings must be the Methodist chapel, which is said to be the oldest octagonal Methodist chapel in continuous use. It dates from 1763 and was visited

Access

Yarm Methodist Chapel is situated in the east side of the township close to Merryweather Court.

Yarm Methodist chapel.

the following year by John Wesley, who preached to a large gathering at five o'clock in the morning. (He described the chapel as 'by far the most elegant in England'.)

Wesley visited Yarm on nineteen occasions between 1748 and 1788, and each time he stayed with George Merryweather at his house, No. 17 High Street. Early meetings were held in a hayloft above stables at the rear of Mr Merryweather's property, and although the hayloft was demolished long ago, inscriptions on two windows of the house quote lines from Young's 'Night Thoughts', and are claimed to be the work of John Wesley.

As Methodist congregations grew in size the hayloft became too small and Mr Merryweather organised the purchase of land for the octagonal chapel (one of fourteen octagonal chapels build in this period). During 1815, the premises were enlarged at a cost of £400 and the original pulpit disappeared without trace. Further alterations in 1873 brought further extensions to this most remarkable church and although the outer walls are the only remaining parts of the original building, the interior has a number of unusual and impressive features.

YARM CASTLE

ARGUABLY THE SMALLEST OF NORTHERN ENGLAND'S MANY CASTLES

The north of England is renowned for its array of mighty castles, but Yarm can surely claim to be home to the smallest of them all. It is possible that an early hill fort covered high ground to the south of the township, but any trace of such an earthwork disappeared long ago and the 'castle' in question is of much more recent vintage.

Access
Commondale House in West Street is privately owned, but the castle and town hall may be viewed from the pavement.

Yarm Castle.

In fact, it is a cement model some 2ft high, dating from 1882 when it was constructed by eighteen-year-old David Doughty who lived in the adjacent Commondale House (opposite the parish church in West Street). A central keep is surrounded by four round towers and a total of more than 800 windows contain all the known gems of the mineral kingdom. These were sometimes illuminated by gas at New Year's Eve or for important events.

A model town hall was added to the wall-top display by David Doughty's son, Henry, in the early 1900s, and other models by the elder Mr Doughty – an abbey ruin and statues of knights in armour – stand in the garden to the rear of the house.

TOM BROWN'S HOUSE, YARM

HOME OF A BRAVE DRAGOON

Access

Tom Brown's House is privately owned and stands on the east side of the High Street between Yarm Bridge and Silver Street.

Yarm's bustling High Street has numerous features of interest and many are highlighted by distinctive plaques and panels. In some cases there is a dramatic story behind a simple statement on an outer wall and this is certainly true of the property known as 'Tom Brown's House'.

Born in Kirkleatham, near Redcar, in 1705, Tom Brown was apprenticed to a shoemaker in Yarm before joining the King's Own Regiment of Dragoons. On 27 June 1743, English forces took part in the battle of Dettingen against a French Army. This rather obscure engagement during the War of Austrian Succession is remembered as the last battle at which a reigning English monarch (George II) led his forces, and it saw Tom Brown become a national hero.

During hostilities French troops captured the regimental standard and, according to reports, Brown charged into enemy ranks and recovered the standard. His bravery resulted in a whole catalogue of injuries, including multiple sabre wounds to his head, face and neck, the loss of two fingers and two musket balls embedded in his back.

After leaving the Army with a pension he returned to Yarm to take over an inn on the east side of Yarm High Street, but he died less than three years later, on 18 January 1746, and was buried in Yarm churchyard. His grave remained unmarked and neglected until

Tom Brown's House on Yarm High Street.

8 June 1969 when his former regiment, now the Queen's Own Hussars, unveiled a memorial stone in his honour close to the east end of the church.

The inn, which became known as Tom Brown's House, lost its licence in 1908, and the weathered signboard was removed a few years ago, leaving only a small, blue plaque to pay tribute to the exploits of this local hero.

Tom Brown's grave in Yarm parish churchyard.

THE DODSHON MEMORIAL

TALES OF A HIGH STREET LANDMARK

Access

Dodshon Memorial occupies a prominent position towards the northern end of Stockton High Street.

Occupying a central position at the northern end of Stockton High Street stands an impressive reminder of a local temperance leader from the Victorian era. The Dodshon Memorial was unveiled for public use during a ceremony led by Joseph Dodds, MP, on 26 August 1878. It was originally sited at the southern end of the High Street (opposite the Exchange Hall) and each of the four sides had a projecting basin with lions' heads cast in bronze, supplying a constant stream of water for use in bronze cups.

Surplus water filled horse and dog troughs at the base, and arched recesses at the higher level were inscribed with details about John Dodshon (born 21 April 1811 and died 20 February 1875), while the topmost sections were decorated with symbolic flowers of the four seasons.

The Dodshon Memorial on Stockton-on-Tees High Street.

At the opening ceremony speakers stressed the value of John Dodshon's work as president of the Temperance Society and, when the official party returned to the town hall to de-robe, local folk rushed to drink from the fountain.

It was undoubtedly the increase in High Street traffic that hastened the memorial's removal to a quieter location on the eastern side of Ropner Park (officially opened by the Duke and Duchess of York on 4 October 1893).

In recent years, changes to the layout of Stockton High Street have facilitated the return of Dodshon's Memorial to a more northerly position.

Left: *Decorative arch on the Dodshon Memorial.*

Below: *Commemorative plaque on the Dodshon Memorial.*

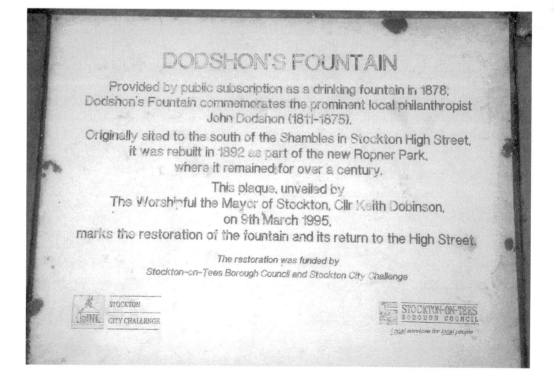

THORNABY AERODROME

FASCINATING CLUES TO A FORMER AIRFIELD SITE

During the last forty years, housing and business premises have spread across much of the former Thornaby aerodrome site, but a number of features remain to provide a fascinating insight into an important chapter of the town's history.

From 1930 to 1958, Thornaby aerodrome was the base for aircraft and aircrews not only from this area but also from countries such as Canada and Australia, and in March 2007 the site was given a dramatic focal point. A full-size replica of a Spitfire was dedicated on 1 April 2007, the anniversary of the formation of the RAF, at the centre of the roundabout on the A1045 Thornaby Road, where it is joined by Bader Avenue and Trenchard Avenue. One side of the Spitfire has the resident 608 Squadron's RAO markings while the other shows the markings of the 401 Squadron Royal Canadian Air Force that flew Spitfires from Thornaby in 1943.

A few hundred yards to the north along Thornaby Road stands the bronze airman's statue, and behind this striking memorial is a much smaller inscribed stone pillar. This was, in fact, an aerodrome boundary marker that was originally positioned at Stainsby Grange Farm.

Further along Thornaby Road stands the much altered Commanding Officer's House (now named Cleveland Lodge) and a terrace of properties that comprised airmen's married quarters. Apart from the date stones on the buildings, closer observation indicates different architectural details and the reason is that the first four terraced properties housed married

Access
Details of Thornaby Aerodrome, then and now, are contained in a leaflet available in local libraries or can be downloaded from the Stockton Borough Council's website at www.stockton. gov.uk

Replica Spitfire on the A1045 Thornaby Road.

airmen while two buildings further along the roadside were occupied by senior Non-Commissioned Officers (NCOs).

The adjoining Martinet Road has the former station headquarters building and, on the opposite side, the NAAFI building, while further along is the drill hall, barrack blocks, Air Ministry works department workshop and original aeroplane shed (dating from 1929).

Nearby, Master Road has the station workshops building (where aeroplane parts and vehicles were repaired), the armoury (with its metal barred windows), and the parachute store.

Other links with the aerodrome site are to be found in street and property names, as well as in St Paul's Church commemorative window, Thornaby Cemetery and the town cenotaph on Acklam Road.

Access

The George and Dragon Inn is located towards the southern end of Yarm High Street.

The building with plaques relating to the railway ticket office is on the south side of the A1130 Bridge Road at Stockton (close to Boathouse Lane). The section of railway embankment runs from the main entrance to Preston Park towards Stockton (beside the A135 Yarm Road).

STOCKTON AND DARLINGTON RAILWAY

LINKS WITH THE EARLY DAYS OF RAIL TRANSPORT

Although it was certainly not this country's first railway, the Stockton and Darlington Railway has found an enduring place in railway history as the first steam-operated public railway carrying freight traffic for reward, and the Tees Valley area has a number of surviving links with this epoch-making enterprise.

Yarm's George and Dragon Inn displays a plaque on an outside wall to highlight the promoters' meeting that took place on 12 February 1820 under the chairmanship of Thomas Meynell. Following this meeting the first rail was laid at Stockton on 23 May 1822 with Meynell taking a leading part, and he also performed the opening ceremony on 27 September 1825.

Probably the best-known landmark on the original route of the Stockton and Darlington Railway is the Skerne Bridge at Darlington, while close to the line's eastern terminus a brick building alongside Bridge Road in Stockton lays claim to housing the ticket office for this pioneering railway line. Another fascinating link with the route is to be found on the edge of Preston Park at Eaglescliffe, where a section of the original railway embankment runs parallel with the A135 Yarm Road.

Above: *George and Dragon Inn, Yarm High Street.*

Right: *Commemorative plaque on the George and Dragon Inn.*

Above: *Tablet on Yarm Town Hall.*

Left: *The original railway embankment of Stockton and Darlington Railway in Preston Park.*

BISHOPTON CASTLE

FACT AND FICTION AT FAIRY HILL

A large, rounded mound on the south side of Bishopton village has featured in both an important episode of north-east history and in the realms of folklore.

Standing some 40ft above surrounding farmland, the motte was adapted from an existing hill during 1143 and represents the best example of an early motte-and-bailey castle in the former County Durham area. It was completed during 1143 on the orders of Roger de Conyers, when a period of civil war affected the neighbourhood.

The castle withstood a siege for several months, but was abandoned when the Conyers family moved their family seat to Sockburn.

An entrance to the castle via a causeway was protected by a small lake that had been created by diverting a nearby stream, and experts suggest that a timber structure on the summit would have been surrounded by a timber palisade.

Folklore maintains that it was a Fairy Hill, and that on one occasion local people ignored a fairy voice's demand that they stop excavations of the mount, and unearthed a locked iron chest. It seemed that they had unearthed the fairies' gold, but when the local blacksmith forced open the 'treasure' chest it contained only a mass of rusty old nails!

In more recent times elder trees have been removed from the summit and have been used for village bonfires. Thankfully, its importance has now been recognised and it is regarded as an ancient monument.

Access

A public footpath passes close to the castle site, which is on the south side of Bishopton village. Bishopton is 4 miles west of Stockton-on-Tees' northern perimeter (via Carlton and Redmarshall).

Bishopton Castle.

STOCKTON GEORGIAN THEATRE

ECHOES FROM THE EARLY DAYS OF ENTERTAINMENT

Access

From Theatre Yard or Green Dragon Yard on the west side of the High Street.

Successive redevelopment schemes have swept away many of Stockton's historic buildings, but on a site adjacent to Theatre Yard there is a remnant of the town's early theatrical history.

Provincial theatre enjoyed a period of prosperity during the eighteenth century, but the country's only purpose-built theatres were to be found in London. Playhouses were usually built to a standard size – measuring about 60ft by 30ft and about 30ft to pitch roof. These were pit and gallery theatres, with boxes added at a later date.

Richmond (North Yorkshire) has a fine fully restored theatre of this type, but the building in Theatre Yard at Stockton is of similar design and even earlier date. It began life as a tithe barn, but was converted to a theatre in 1766 by Thomas Bates, manager of a company of comedians.

For some twenty years the theatre prospered as one of a number of venues in North Yorkshire and South Durham that were visited by Bates' touring company, but during 1786 ownership passed to James Cawdell, a well-known actor from the period. He inherited considerable debts from Thomas Bates but soon showed himself to be a successful businessman and made sizeable profits from his theatrical interests. In 1898 he rented the Stockton Theatre to Stephen Kemble, a member of the famous theatrical family, but neither Kemble nor a succession of other owners made it pay as well as Cawdell.

Stephen Kemble made his farewell appearance as Falstaff on 6 July 1815. He had made improvements to the building, and in 1818 there were further alterations when Anderson and Faulkner installed boxes. There are few details about the succession of owners during the next forty years but it is known that one of the last companies to appear at the theatre (in 1861) was Mr Powell's Leicester Players.

During the 1850s it was known as the 'Royal', but by this time music halls were becoming the most popular form of entertainment in the north of England and the theatre was soon to degenerate into the 'Oxford Music Hall'. The building was later converted for use as a Salvation Army headquarters and then became a sweet factory. During the 1970s, Stockton Council carried out restoration work on the premises and in recent years it has again staged musical concerts and theatrical occasions.

Inscribed tablet on the wall of Stockton's Georgian theatre.

Access

The millennium sculpture is in the centre of the grassy area on the south-west side of Wolviston.

WOLVISTON GREEN MILLENNIUM SCULPTURE

A FEATURE WITH A DIFFERENCE

From colourful church windows to dramatic roadside crosses, millennium sculptures take many forms but one of the most innovative and attractive must be the metal feature at the centre of Wolviston Green.

A simple plaque explains that the gold-painted hands on both sides of three open panels represent children's creative thoughts for the millennium. The work was commissioned by Wolviston Parish Council and the sculptor, Len Horsey. Some hands show simple drawings while others have simple statements such as 'Best Friends Forever' and 'Mrs Happy'.

From a distance the sculpture is attractive and unusual while closer inspection reveals any amount of warmth and humanity.

Wolviston Green Millennium Sculpture.

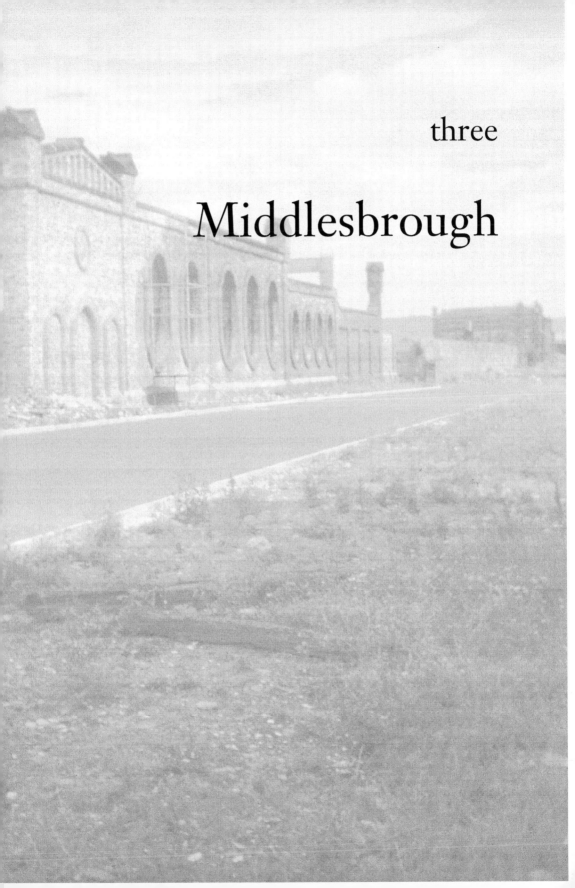

three

Middlesbrough

THE WHITE STAG

A STRIKING BUSINESS SCULPTURE

Access

The White Stag is clearly visible from Linthorpe Road on the roof line opposite St Barnabas Road.

Properties along the southern end of Linthorpe Road are still known by many local people as 'Linthorpe Village'. Roof lines and frontages hold many interesting features, but perhaps the best known is the stag.

There is no evidence to explain when it was initially placed on the first-floor roof, but it may date to the Edwardian period. Initially, it was known as the 'Golden Hind', but later it was renamed the 'White Stag'. During the Second World War the stag was painted black, but by 2003 it was again a golden colour. Following repair work in 2007 this fine sculpture has been painted white.

The White Stag on business premises opposite St Barnabas Road, Linthorpe.

The building upon which the stag is positioned is recorded in the 1860s as Simpson House, and it continued to be a private residence into the 1890s, when the last occupant was James Lawrence Busch, proprietor of J.L. Busch & Co., shipowners, with offices at No. 97 Lower Commercial Street.

By 1897, the premises had changed from residential to business use and it was soon divided into two separate shops.

In 1900 Mrs A.M. Roe, wine and spirit merchant, was in business at No. 16, while a draper, Mr J. Armstrong, was based at No. 16a. Directories for 1904 show that Winterschladen & Co. Ltd, wine and spirit merchants, had taken over with Mr A.L. Roe as manager and by 1913 this company owned the whole building as one complete shop. It is quite possible that the stag was placed on its roof-top position at this time.

Winterschladen & Co. Ltd stayed at the premises for some eighty-five years before it became Parker Stag Estate Agency in 1990. The building is currently rented from MZ Factoring and MZ Trading by Drummonds Estate Agency.

NEWHAM BRIDGE (DEVIL'S BRIDGE)

FACT OR FOLKLORE ON MIDDLESBROUGH'S SOUTHERN PERIMETER

Until housing developments spread southwards along Middlesbrough's boundaries in the late twentieth century, Acklam retained much of its rural character. First mentioned in the Domesday Book of 1086, the community was later dominated by the Hustler family's magnificent residence, Acklam Hall, but close by is a structure of much humbler origins – Newham Bridge.

Spanning Marton West Beck close to its confluence with Newham Beck, this humble stone bridge became known locally as 'Devil's Bridge' through the imprint of a cloven hoof on one of its stones.

The north of England has any number of similarly named bridges where local folklore links the devil to unfortunate incidents that befall

Newham Bridge, known locally as Devil's Bridge.

unwary travellers, and Newham Bridge must rank as one of the smallest
of this collection.

Yet this simple structure may hold an amount of interest through
possible links with early routes in the area. Although there is no firm
evidence to connect Roman Road in the Linthorpe area with early
highways, Ladgate Lane is also singled out as an ancient roadway
from the Pennines to the east coast, and there are clear signs of an
early route to the south of Thornaby. Recent discoveries of Roman-
British settlements in the Ingleby Barwick and Marton areas could well
be linked to the section of roadway that runs in an east-west direction
close to Thornaby's Low Wood. Future discoveries may yet forge a link
between Devil's Bridge at Acklam and these early thoroughfares.

VIKING, WITCH AND MONK SILHOUETTES

GHOSTLY FIGURES WITH LOCAL LINKS

Middlesbrough's longest beck, Marton West Beck, runs from Albert Park to the countryside on the town's southern boundary, with a range of habitats for plant, animal and bird life along its meandering route. In recent years the addition of steel sculptures has highlighted aspects of local history and folklore linked with this fascinating location.

At the northern end of the beck, in Albert Park, there is the outline of a horseman and, just south of the A174 (Parkway), the silhouette of a Viking warrior stands close to the ancient settlement of Tollesby, which can trace its origins back to pre-Norman times.

Mature woodland and ponds in Fairy Dell provide a habitat for mallards, coots and moorhens, while celandines, wood avens and dog's mercury cover the ground around the metallic figure of a witch on her

Access

The figures are located alongside Marton West Beck between Albert Park and Brass Castle Lane.

Silhouettes beside Morton West Beck.

The witch silhouette at Fairy Dell.

broomstick. Local folklore suggests that a witch would not cross running water in pursuit of a potential victim.

Further south, Marton West Beck runs close to Brass Castle Lane where the figure of a monk is said to mark the boundary of lands held by local priories.

FIVE TELEPHONE BOXES

AN UNUSUAL NUMBER OF KIOSKS (BEHIND MIDDLESBROUGH TOWN HALL)

Middlesbrough's rapid growth during the late Victorian period saw the construction of a number of imposing commercial, civic and public buildings on land south of the

Access

The telephone kiosks stand on the pavement on the north side of Dunning Road at the rear of Middlesbrough town hall.

town's railway station. Land at the corner of Corporation Road and Albert Road was chosen as the site for Middlesbrough's new town hall and municipal buildings, and the foundation stone was laid on 24 October 1883. The official opening was carried out by the Prince and Princess of Wales (the future King Edward VII and Queen Alexandra) at a ceremony held on 23 January 1887.

The dominant feature of George Gordon Hoskins' scheme was a clock tower measuring 170ft in height, but another highly unusual aspect of the municipal complex is often overlooked. Lining the roadside at the rear of the town hall (on Dunning Road) is a row of five original red-painted telephone boxes. They have probably survived successive phases of town centre modernisation because of the town hall's listed status, but a wartime air raid almost caused their demise. A bomb fell about 40yds away at the other corner of the town hall, causing damage to public toilets on Corporation Road and shrapnel struck the main building.

The five telephone boxes behind Middlesbrough Town Hall.

FEATURES FROM THORNTON HALL

CLUES TO A LONG-LOST MANSION

Access

Stonework features and the tree section are all to be found along the stretch of Thornton Road, running south to the junction with Seamer Road.

Ormesby Hall is well known as the former family home of the Pennyman family, but few people realise that the Pennymans also owned another mansion, Thornton Hall, on Middlesbrough's southern boundary. The only known record of this building seems to be a sketch by Samuel Buck dating from about 1720, when it was owned by James Pennyman.

By the end of the eighteenth century this substantial property had disappeared, seemingly without trace. Yet in the locality there are tantalising clues to Thornton Hall's impressive features. Stone gateposts beside the steps leading from Thornton Road into the churchyard of St Peter and St Paul's at Stainton and similar gateposts at the nearby property, 'Red Walls', have been identified as originating from Thornton Hall.

Further along Thornton Road, at the junction with Seamer Road, Thornton Low Farm has any number of intriguing features. Pilasters and pediments around doors and windows are not usually found in vernacular farm buildings and the clear indication is that they once

Thornton Low Farm, near the site of Thornton Hall.

graced the frontage of nearby Thornton Hall. Other parts of the farm building are said to be from the Old Hall at Stainsby, near Thornaby, former home of the Gower family. It is also believed that many of the Pennyman estate cottages were built of bricks from the hall.

The grounds around Thornton Hall were dominated by an enormous Cedar of Lebanon tree with a girth of 13ft 4in. Following the demolition of the hall, the tree remained in place and in 1890 it was referred to as the 'finest known specimen in England'. Its demise came in 1962 when gale-force winds brought it crashing down, but a section of trunk was salvaged and positioned close to the junction of Thornton Road and Seamer Road.

BLACK POPLAR (*POPULUS NIGRA BETULIFOLIA*)

A RARE FEMALE OF THE SPECIES

There can be few more majestic sights than a mature tree in a prominent position, and when the tree is one of few in number then it gains even more significance.

Throughout the whole country there are probably a total of a few hundred native black poplars (*Populus Nigra Betulifolia*), but only a handful of these are the female of the species. One of these rare specimens covers ground outside the College of Art building close to the junction of Green Lane and Roman Road.

It is estimated to be around 140 years old and such trees may live for about 300 years. The black poplars' branches hang down like a weeping willow and in medieval times they were used to build cruck houses. More recently, these thin branches were used to make packing cases or artificial limbs, and its slow-burning properties have led to its use in making matches and artificial wooden limbs.

The black poplars' natural habitat is a flood plain and they are not easy to propagate, though the junction of Green Lane and Roman Road is festooned each June by seeds from this impressive tree.

It is speculated that this black poplar was planted at this location by the owner of the large property that previously stood on the site, and, along with a specimen in Darlington, it lays claim to being the most northerly black poplar in England.

Access

The black poplar is clearly visible from roadside pavements along Green Lane, close to the junction with Roman Road.

FORMER NATIONAL PROVINCIAL BANK

DOORS DEPICTING ANCIENT COIN MOTIFS

Middlesbrough's importance as a business and shopping centre means that its streets are usually thronged with people and traffic, and it is easy to overlook some of the town's fine Victorian and Edwardian architecture.

Access

The doors of No. 37 Albert Road are at the front of the building, now housing the Barracuda Club, and are clearly visible from the roadside.

Left: *Black Poplar outside the College of Art building on Green Lane.*

Below: *The doors of the former National Provinsial Bank (left), and plaque (right).*

It is often the upper levels and roof lines of buildings that attract attention, but in the case of No. 37 Albert Road the doors of the main entrance are the focus of interest.

Opened as the National Provincial Bank building in 1939, the doors were commissioned from the Birmingham Guild Ltd, and were probably designed by W.H. Holden, the National Provincial's Chief Architect between 1935 and 1947. The two doors have a total of twenty-four panels, showing motifs on ancient coins originating in the Mediterranean area.

An inscription on the bronze tablet on the left-hand door frame explains the origins and date of each motif, and the coin department of the British Museum was consulted in order to ensure their historical accuracy.

The premises were converted to a bar, the Club Zantia, in 1997, and a further change of name now sees it operate under the name Barracuda.

OUTDOOR ITEMS AT THE DORMAN MUSEUM

FROM ROMAN SARCOPHAGUS TO SAILORS TROD

In recent years Middlesbrough's Dorman Museum has been extended and updated to include a range of displays relating to aspects of the town's history. (Officially opened by Col J. Hoole, Commanding Officer of the 3rd Yorkshire Regiment on 1 July 1904, the building had been financed by Sir A.J. Dorman as a memorial to his son, Lt G.L. Dorman, and members of the Green Howards who died in the South African War).

Most visitors are drawn to the fascinating exhibitions within the museum and it is easy to overlook items that are located in the grounds of the building. Close to the perimeter railings stands a splendid sarcophagus which was excavated by workmen at the Northamptonshire premises of the Cargo Fleet Iron Co. Ltd. Further investigation revealed that the limestone coffin was within the Roman township of Irchester and it was donated to the Dorman Museum in 1926.

On the other side of the central pathway lies a large stone boulder which is reported to have been originally sited in the wide, shallow channel of the Tees at Newport. Until a bridge was completed between Stockton and Thornaby in 1769, Yarm bridge represented the lowest

Access

Items are located in front of the main entrance to the Dorman Museum and on the north side of the main walkway in Albert Park.

crossing point on the Tees and a ford and stepping stones in the vicinity of Newport offered an alternative for travellers.

The nearby Albert Park was officially opened by Prince Arthur of Connaught on 11 August 1868 and was named after his father (the husband of Queen Victoria). Parts of the park have recently been restyled, but on the north side of the main avenue there is a feature from Middlesbrough's earlier days. Lines of hawthorn trees are said to have marked the ancient 'sailors' trod' used by sea-going men travelling to and from staging posts along the River Tees. (Intriguingly, a hawthorn tree behind the pavilion on the north side of the main walkway has a piece of ironstone lodged in the crook of the branches. Known as 'The Message Tree', this particular hawthorn is claimed to have been used by sailors to leave messages.)

Roman coffin sited outside the Dorman Museum.

The boulder which was said to have been a stepping stone across the Tees at Newport.

RUSSIAN CANNON IN ALBERT PARK

A MUCH-TRAVELLED ARTILLERY PIECE

During the Crimean War some 700 cannons were captured from Russian forces and a number of them were offered to 'such cities or towns in Britain and Ireland as have proper place to put them'. The Victorian boom town of Middlesbrough was made an offer and council minutes, dated 8 December 1857, document the decision to 'accept Lord Panmure's [Secretary of State for War] present of a Russian iron gun'.

The cannon was transported to Middlesbrough during the summer of 1858 on board *The Advance*, the first iron-built ship on the Tees, and the decision was made to station it in St Hilda's churchyard. Eight years later it was moved to a position overlooking a lake on land that was later to be landscaped as Albert Park.

Access

The cannon occupies a prominent position beside the northern edge of the central walkway.

Russian cannon in Albert Park.

Until 1946, this fine artillery piece, a 25-pounder iron gun which fired a 6in ball, stood beside Cannon Lake, but when the decision was taken to fill in the lake it was moved to Stewart Park.

After years of neglect, the cannon's plight was highlighted by the local media in 1965, and following repair work it was installed on a concrete base outside the Stockton Road Drill Hall. Changes in the road system meant that it would remain largely unnoticed in that location and in 1978 it was agreed that P. Battery of the DLI should return it to the care of Middlesbrough Council. During September 1978 it was positioned outside the Dorman Museum.

The most recent move has seen this impressive item of military history located on the north side of the central walkway in Albert Park.

MIDDLESBROUGH DOCK TOWER

MYSTERY SURROUNDING A MISSING CLOCK FACE

First opened on 12 May 1842 with an area of water covering 9 acres, Middlesbrough Dock was extended in 1869, 1885 and 1895 to give a total of over 25 acres with ten berths, but following its closure in the summer of 1980 many of the dockside features have been removed.

Access

The tower is clearly visible from Scott's Road (across the entrance channel from Middlesbrough FC's Riverside Stadium).

Middlesbrough Dock Tower.

The northern end of the dock is dominated by the four-storey dock tower which is in direct line with Vulcan Street. An earlier tower stood on the east side of the dock, close to the lock gates and had a gallery with a balustrade to allow it to serve as a lookout point for vessels entering and leaving the dock. The spire of St Hilda's Church, in the town's central market place, served a similar navigational function.

There is uncertainty about the present tower's date of construction. It may date from around 1870, but as the original structure lasted for some thirty years after this date it is likely that the current tower was constructed at the end of the nineteenth century. Tall and elegant with red-brick walls, highlighted by terracotta dressings and a slate roof,

Middlesbrough Dock Tower.

the tower has only three clock faces. There are several suggestions for the lack of a fourth clock face, including a shortage of cash resources to finish the work and a desire to prevent riverside workers from clock watching. Another theory states that the owners of Bolckow & Vaughan's Ironworks on Vulcan Street or Railton Dixon's premises would not contribute to the cost of installing a clock on the fourth side, and so it remained blank.

In 1988 the dock tower was given Grade II* rating in the List of Buildings of Special Architectural or Historical Interest. Demolition of recent extensions to the tower and a thorough programme of clearing and restorations have preserved this splendid structure in its original form.

SALTWORKS WALL ON THE SITE OF AN EARLY IRONWORKS

A FRAGMENT OF MIDDLESBROUGH'S EARLY INDUSTRIAL HISTORY

In recent years Middlesbrough's riverside sector has seen dramatic phases of demolition and redevelopment leaving few reminders of the town's early industrial development. Yet almost within the shadow of the Transporter Bridge there is a striking link with those early pioneering industries.

It was in this locality that Middlesbrough Pottery's first kiln was fired in April 1834 with the first export to Gibraltar leaving the Tees some five months later. The pottery's main period of prosperity was in the early 1850s and just a few years earlier, in 1841, iron-making got underway close to Vulcan Street.

A section of brick wall from the Cleveland Salt Co.'s premises on the north side of Vulcan Street runs alongside the site of this early Bolckow and Vaughan ironworks. When a shaft was sunk on 4 July 1859 it seems probable that the plan was to locate seams of coal but salt was discovered in 1863. Further investigations took place in the late 1860s, and in 1887 the Cleveland Salt Co. took over operations. They extracted salt as a brine solution and production continued for more than sixty years.

Access

The section of brick wall runs alongside the northern edge of Vulcan Street (across the road from the site of Middlesbrough Pottery).

Saltworks wall on the northern side of Vulcan Street.

BELLS OF ST HILDA'S CHURCH

MUSICAL SURVIVORS FROM MIDDLESBROUGH'S FIRST ANGLICAN CHURCH

Access

The campanile and bells occupy a central position on Grange Road, close to the junction with Linthorpe Road.

Few of Middlesbrough's early buildings have survived successive phases of redevelopment and perhaps the saddest loss was St Hilda's Church, which was demolished in 1969.

The foundation stone of this fine, early English-style building was laid during July 1838 and overall costs totalled £2,500. Consecrated on 25 September 1840, there was seating for 600 worshippers and the architect was J.B. Green of Newcastle-on-Tyne. The western tower initially contained a single bell that was made by Mears Stainbeck of

Church Bell Foundry in London, but in 1864 a peal of eight bells was added. Cast in bronze by Mears and Stainbeck, they were inscribed with details of local ironmasters who had funded their manufacture.

Following the demolition of St Hilda's in 1969, the bells were stored and then hung in a campanile on the south side of All Saints' Church (on the corner of Linthorpe Road and Grange Road). A further move has seen them transferred to a more prominent site on Grange Road, close to the Linthorpe Road junction where a series of inscribed discs set in the pavement below the campanile give details of the bells' fascinating origins.

Campanile and bells of St Hilda's Church on Grange Road.

The Custom House on North Street.

CUSTOM HOUSE

CLASSICAL STYLE IN AN INDUSTRIAL HEARTLAND

Access

The Custom House is on North Street close to the junction with Commercial Street.

Middlesbrough is renowned for its dramatic industrial growth as a Victorian boom town and it is appropriate that the only Greek-revival-style building in this 'infant Hercules' has survived to take on an alternative role in the twenty-first century.

The splendid six-bayed building on North Street opened as Middlesbrough's first exchange and also provided accommodation as a hotel. During the following year it was the setting for a reception held in honour of the Duke of Sussex, who was the uncle of Queen Victoria and the first member of the royal family to visit the burgeoning township.

From the 1850s it was used as an annex to the nearby Old Town Hall before being taken over to serve as a Custom House in 1886. In more recent years this fine building, with two Greek Doric-style columns flanking the entrance, has served as a community centre and as the original heartland of Middlesbrough is redeveloped it stands proudly awaiting a future role.

NEWPORT LIFT BRIDGE

AN INNOVATIVE EXAMPLE OF BRIDGE DESIGN

Access

Tees Newport
Bridge carries
the A1032
road from
the Newport
Interchange
(south side)
to Portrack
Interchange
(north side).

Low-lying river banks and the need to allow the passage of sea-going vessels accounts for the unusual design features of two bridges along lower stretches of the Tees. A little distance downstream the Transporter Bridge has a travelling car, while the later bridge between Newport and Portrack was constructed with a central section that lifted high above the river.

Designed by Mott, Hay and Anderson, it was built by Dorman Long Ltd – the firm that also constructed the Tyne and Sydney Harbour bridges – and became the first vertical-lift bridge to be constructed in this country.

Opened on 28 February 1934 by His Royal Highness, the Duke of York, the lifting or lowering operation was completed in approximately 1½ minutes and for a number of years an average of 800 vessels per week passed under the bridge. However, during the summer of 1989, a bill passed through Parliament to allow the bolting down of the bridge (in order to save maintenance and replacement costs).

On the northern approach to the Newport Bridge – the A1032 – traffic crosses the Billingham Branch Line Bridge. Designed by Sir Gilbert Roberts, the five-spanned 226ft bridge was the country's first welded bridge and represented a major step in bridge construction by using techniques since copied in many later bridges.

*Newport Lift Bridge,
viewed from the south.*

THE TRANSPORTER BRIDGE

SYMBOL OF TEESSIDE – AN AMAZING 'FLYING FERRY'

Access

The Transporter Bridge can be reached from Ferry Road (north of Middlesbrough railway station) or from the A178 at Port Clarence (north bank). A visitor centre is open on the southern approach Monday-Saturday 9 a.m.-5 p.m., and Sunday 2 p.m.-5 p.m.

Curiosities do not come much larger than the Transporter Bridge, which spans the Tees between Middlesbrough and Port Clarence. With a total length of 851ft (259.3m), it is the longest remaining transporter bridge in the world, and has a maximum height above high water of 225ft (69m).

A ferry service across the Tees was introduced in 1907 and when an act of Parliament was obtained in the same year for construction of a bridge, the scheme was approved on condition that river navigation was not affected. This consideration explains the design in which a travelling car (or gondola) is suspended on steel cables and runs on a wheel and rail system between towers on either side of the river.

Sir William Arrol & Co. Ltd of Glasgow were awarded the contract for building the bridge at a cost of £68,026 6s 8d. The foundation stones of Aberdeen granite were laid by Middlesbrough's Mayor, Lt-Col T. Gibson Poole, and Alderman Joseph McLauchlan, who had proposed the whole project in 1910, and on 17 October 1911 the bridge was officially opened by Prince Arthur of Connaught.

A quarter-hourly service for up to 600 people or an equivalent load of vehicles has continued since 1911, with a crossing time of around 2½ minutes. This regular service, for eighteen hours a day, has been interrupted only for routine maintenance, and at times for lengthier major repairs and refurbishment schemes.

During the Second World War the superstructure was hit by a bomb and in 1953 the carriage was stranded mid-river while gale force winds lashed water to within inches of it, but this amazing feat of civil engineering has survived to attract worldwide interest.

In 1985 the bridge was given Grade II* listed building status, and during 1993 flood lights were added for operating in the winter months. Since 1996, ownership of the bridge has been shared by Middlesbrough Council and Stockton-on-Tees Borough Council, with the former in charge of day-to-day operations and maintenance.

Heading towards its centenary, the Transporter Bridge remains as an instantly recognisable landmark on the lower reaches of the Tees and as a symbol of the dynamic industrial growth that created much of modern Teesside.

Transporter Bridge.

four

Hartlepool

88

FIGUREHEAD FROM *THE RISING SUN*

DRAMATIC RELIC FROM A VICTIM OF THE STORM

Access

The figurehead is displayed on the frontage of the White Hart Inn, which stands on the north side of Front Street in Hart Village.

Down the years countless vessels have foundered along the north-east coast and many of these went down in Hartlepool Bay. All too often the villain of the piece was a savage north-east gale, and in many places figureheads from stricken vessels served as a sobering reminder of the tragic loss of lives.

Few figureheads remain in the area, but in Hart village the White Hart Inn displays a figurehead from a barque, *The Rising Sun*, which was one of sixty ships wrecked in 1861.

Figurehead from The Rising Sun *on the front wall of the White Hart Inn.*

The White Hart Inn.

FRIARY MANSION (OR MANOR HOUSE)

AN INTRIGUING LINK WITH A FRANCISCAN FRIARY

In the medieval period, the township on Hartlepool's Headland area would have been overshadowed by St Hilda's Church and buildings linked with the friary church. The impressive stonework of St Hilda's remains intact but almost every trace of nearby friarage buildings have gone.

The medieval Franciscan friary was closed by Henry VIII's commissioners in 1536 and parts of the site were later covered by hospital buildings and Henry Smith's Grammar School. In recent years these premises have also been demolished, but a curious structure has survived from those early days.

Dating from the late sixteenth century, the Manor House, or 'The Friarage' as it is sometimes known, is believed to have been constructed with materials from the original monastery. At one time it served as a poor house and in later times it was incorporated into the buildings of St Hilda's Hospital. (During this phase nursing staff reported sightings of a 'grey lady' or possibly 'grey friar' around the site.)

Access

The Friary Mansion stands on ground to the east of Friar Street on Hartlepool Headland.

The Friary Mansion, East Street, on Hartlepool Headland.

Following phases of demolition and redevelopment this fascinating building stands in isolation while future phases of the Headland Regeneration Scheme are formulated.

THE HARTLEPOOL MONKEY

A TOWN'S BEST-KNOWN LEGEND

Access

The monkey figure is located in Union Dock close to Navigation Point Shopping and Hotel Centre.

Hartlepool Headland has a rich and varied heritage which includes links with the Abbess Hilda, through a Saxon monastery and the mighty de Brus family, who were based at nearby Hart during the medieval period.

In more recent times, Hartlepool has become well known for its monkey legend. Set in the early nineteenth century when there was a widespread fear of invasion by Napoleonic forces, a raft was washed ashore during stormy weather. Although it was suggested by wiser

Monkey statue in Union Dock.

counsel that the sole occupant of the raft was a monkey, the consensus among the crowd of onlookers was that it must be a French spy. A mock trial was arranged and when the stranger was subjected to questioning its babbling response was taken as proof of its guilt. The unfortunate castaway was condemned to die for treason and a gibbet was set up on the Fish Sands.

Similar stores are told around other parts of Britain, including Cornwall and Bodiam in Aberdeenshire, where local wreckers lured a ship on to the rocks. The ship's monkey was the only survivor, but it was promptly hanged by the wrecking party so that they could claim the cargo.

The Hartlepool episode was popularised during the 1950s by a north-east entertainer, Ned Corvan, who wrote a song called 'The Fishermen Hung the Monkey O'. It was probably based on a song from Tyneside called 'The Baboon', which was published in 1827, and described the pursuit of a baboon, dressed in uniform, by local pitmen. It had escaped from a travelling menagerie, but locals believed it was a French spy. Ned Corvan performed the song for the first time at Dock Street Musical Hall in Hartlepool and the town was very quickly recognised as the setting for the monkey legend. One of the town's rugby teams, Hartlepool

Rovers, focused attention on the legend by hanging a stuffed monkey from the crossbar before each match during the 1890s. They even took it on tour with the team, where the story attracted coverage from national newspapers.

THE MEDIEVAL TOWN WALL AT HARTLEPOOL

EARLY DEFENCES FOR AN IMPORTANT COASTAL BASE

Access

The town wall runs from the Fish Sands to the Fish Quay at the seaward end of Northgate (A1049) on Hartlepool Headland.

A section of Hartlepool's medieval town wall still runs along the southern flank of the Headland where it serves as a sea wall. Most of the original length of the wall has long since disappeared, but the surviving portion gives an indication of Hartlepool's importance during a period of border warfare in the early fourteenth century.

Hartlepool acted as an important supply port for English armies and a safe refuge for the fleet. The walls enclosed the whole of the medieval town, the Franciscan friary and the harbour as well as a large area of the town fields. Entrances through the wall were made at Northgate and probably Durham Street, as well as at the harbour opening.

Excavations at other places on the line of the wall indicate that the construction of the wall with limestone blocks was preceded by a huge ditch, measuring 5m in width and more than 4m in depth.

A series of round and square towers were added to the wall in two phases, with round towers dating from the early fourteenth century and square towers added in the late 1300s. It is thought that Sandwell Gate, which overlooks the Fish Sands, was built into the wall at this later date.

Plans for replacement walls were probably prepared in 1639, after Sir Thomas Merton viewed the state of defences and concluded that the medieval walls had fallen away in many places. Work on new defensive measures, he reported, would require charges and time to carry out repairs. Upheaval during the English Civil War period and the expense involved probably account for the failure to make the planned changes and, ironically, Scottish forces occupied the township for three years from 1644.

Medieval town walls and Sandwell Gate.

Town walls and St Hilda's Church.

THE SHADES

ART NOUVEAU STYLE IN AN URBAN SETTING

Access

The Shades is located on the south side of Church Street (A178) between Church Square and Mainsforth Terrace.

In recent years, schemes such as the development of the Historic Quay and Marina, restoration of Ward Jackson Park and phases of Headland Regeneration have restored much of Hartlepool's earlier glory. Areas of the town centre have seen modernisation schemes, but amid the upgrading there are artistic features from previous times.

Church Street is lined with business and leisure premises, including 'The Shades' which dates from the early years of the twentieth century. The building's exterior displays a wonderfully exuberant Art Nouveau style featuring rows of dancing girls.

Many towns have licensed premises with facades of ceramic tiles but few, if any, can equal this superb frontage. The style even continues along the side of the building where characteristic Art Nouveau lettering reads, 'Jug and Bottle'.

The Shades on the south side of Church Street.

CHRIST CHURCH

*IMPRESSIVE DIMENSIONS OF AN UNUSUAL
VICTORIAN PLACE OF WORSHIP*

Numbered among Hartlepool's collection of fine church buildings
are two outstanding examples of very different styles of architecture.
St Hilda's is a superb example of the Early English style, with a
whole array of flying buttresses supporting the massive weight of the
thirteenth-century church.

In total contrast, Christ Church in Church Square, at the western
end of the town's Church Street, has all the characteristics of an
unorthodox Victorian architect. Ralph Ward Jackson, founder of West
Hartlepool, wanted a new church for his developing township and he
set up an architectural competition which was won by the London-
based architect, Edward Buckton Lamb.

Christ Church was constructed in the Early English style of the
Gothic revival, with stone recovered from excavations for the Jackson
Dock and wooden altar rails including sections of prehistoric 'bog oak'.
It is the dimensions of the church which are really out of the ordinary,

Access

Christ Church
dominates
Church Square
at the western
end of Church
Street in West
Hartlepool.

Christ Church in Church Square.

with a tower at the west end soaring 100ft from the ground, and a spire on the tower's south-east corner adding another 25ft. With a mixture of different architectural periods, the tower seems unbalanced and over-powering yet totally absorbing and appropriate. By comparison, the main body of the church is extremely low, and on the inside the unconventional aspects are on show again with an array of bristling roof timbers.

Consecrated for worship on 20 April 1854 at a cost of £8,000, this highly unusual church saw a decline in congregations after the Second World War and it was closed in April 1974. For the next nineteen years it was used as a store before being renovated at a cost of £2,000,000.

On 5 January 1996, Christ Church reopened as an art gallery and tourist information centre.

DE BRUS WALL

A FASCINATING REMINDER OF A FORMIDABLE NORTHERN FAMILY

Access

The de Brus Wall is accessible from the A179 Hart Road via Butts Lane and Magdalene Drive on the west side of Hart Church

During the twelfth and thirteenth centuries the de Brus family were a powerful force in the Tees area. A total of eight successive members were named Robert, and Robert de Brus II founded Guisborough Priory in the early twelfth century before commanding troops at the Battle of the Standard in 1138.

The de Brus family were largely responsible for the growth of Hartlepool in the thirteenth century on the rocky peninsula now known as Hartlepool Headland, but it is the nearby village of Hart that holds a fascinating reminder of this daunting northern family.

A section of stone wall runs alongside an open area of ground to the west of St Mary Magdalene's Church, which is known as the de Brus Wall. It represents the remnant of a building dating from the Norman period when it was the base for the de Brus family. Local speculation claims it was the birthplace of Robert de Brus who later became King of Scotland.

The de Brus Wall, to the west of St Mary Magdalene's Church.

HARTLEPOOL'S SUBMERGED FOREST

NEOLITHIC REMAINS ON THE SEASHORE

Down the centuries County Durham's coastline has seen constant changes, but one of the oldest features is to be found on Hartlepool's foreshore, where an amazing submerged forest stretches for about 400yds to the north and south of Newburn Bridge. Its importance has seen this incredible location designated as a Site of Special Scientific Interest.

Thousands of years ago this area had a totally different appearance, with a covering of trees and peat bog. In about 8000 BC there was a land bridge linking Britain with the rest of Europe and much of the modern North Sea was low-level fenland.

During 1971 a Neolithic male skeleton was uncovered from the site and experts estimate that the man was aged between twenty-five and thirty-five years old when he was laid on the peat bed in a crouching position on his right side. A small collection of flint flakes had been placed close to his elbow and there was evidence that the body had been covered with branches and twigs of birch.

Access

Hartlepool beach is accessible from Coronation Drive (A178) between Newburn Bridge and Seaton Carew.

Sea-defence work facilitated close inspection of the forest during 1990, 1995 and 2002, and this resulted in identification of lines of wooden stakes and worked flints. Erosion of surface peat in 1984 exposed over 2yds of wattle hurdling, and after removal and conservation by Durham University scientists these items were radio carbon dated to 3600 BC and identified as part of a fish trap.

THROSTON ENGINE HOUSE

DRAMATIC INDUSTRIAL RELIC

A fine stone building with classical features that overlooks a busy junction in the Throston area could easily be mistaken for an example of nineteenth-century domestic architecture. In fact, it is one of the area's most attractive early nineteenth-century industrial buildings, and although there is no trace of coal staithes, railway lines and bridge, this imposing structure serves as a dramatic reminder of the days

Throston Engine House.

when loaded coal wagons were hauled up an inclined slope adjacent to Throston Bridge by a fixed steam engine in the engine house.

It is believed to date from about 1834, as the first coal shipments from Thornley took place in 1835 and the building is shown on Mossman's survey of 1851. Coal was carried over the nearby bridge to staithes in the harbour, but the engine house became redundant in the 1850s after the rapid expansion of the West Hartlepool Docks.

ST HILDA'S CHURCHYARD

CLUES TO PERSONALITIES FROM A TOWN'S PAST

Many churchyards house a fascinating collection of memorials with a whole range of headstones and monuments offering an insight into the part played by major personalities, and ordinary people, in the development of their district.

Christopher Tennant played a major part in developing the local railway network. He pioneered the opening of the Stockton and Hartlepool Railway during 1839 but died in September of that year.

Another grave in St Hilda's churchyard marks the final resting place of 'Caesar'. Baptised in St Hilda's Church in 1750, he was the slave of a local merchant.

During the mid-nineteenth century, groups of travelling showmen added colour and excitement to northern towns. Numbered among them was Billy

The grave of Billy Purvis in St Hilda's churchyard.

Access

St Hilda's
Church and
churchyard
are on the east
side of the
Town Square
on Hartlepool
Headland.

Purvis, who was widely regarded as one of the finest English clowns, and he was at the height of his popularity during the autumn of 1852. His act usually included Celtic dances, puppets, a clog hornpipe and a finale based on the farce *Mesmerism* or *The Days of Dupes*.

Purvis died on 16 December 1853 and was buried in St Hilda's churchyard along with numerous other characters from the locality.

five

Darlington

GLACIAL BOULDER AT SADBERGE

LINKS WITH A VILLAGE'S IMPORTANT PAST

Access

The boulder is positioned on open grassland on the south-west side of the crossroads in the centre of Sadberge.

Erratics (glacial boulders) can be found in many locations throughout the north-east of England. Brought down from the Pennine Range during the Ice Age, some have been arranged in neat rows during farming work. (A collection of such boulders line footpaths south of the Tees between Barnard Castle and Eggleston Abbey.)

In some places single boulders have been set up for display purposes. A prominent grey boulder at the centre of Sadberge village green has a brass plate with the inscription that states:

> This stone was placed here to commemorate the jubilee of Victoria, Queen of the United Kingdom, Empress of India and Countess of Sadberge, June 20 1887. It was found 12ft below the surface in making the reservoir. It had been detached from the rock in the west and deposited by a glacier.

It offers a clue to Sadberge's early importance at the heart of the Wapentake of Sadberge, where important trade routes crossed. The presence of a castle and assizes court also serve to emphasise the community's strategic and legislative importance.

The boulder with commemorative plaque on Sadberge village green.

YARDS AND WYNDS

NARROW ROADWAYS AND LINKS WITH A MIGHTY BEAST

Access
Bull Wynd
connects
Horsemarket
and Houndgate
to the south-
west of the
market hall.

Darlington's yards and wynds are a long-established feature of the modern town centre settings. Each of these historic thoroughfares adds an amount of interest and atmosphere to the area between Houndgate and Northgate.

The best-known of these routes, Post House Wynd, has been developed as a popular shopping route, and Clark's Yard retains its original 'finkle' – meaning bend-along with other early features. Bull Wynd's narrow roadway links the Horsemarket with Houndgate, and high up on a wall at the northern end is a stone tablet showing a bull with a 'shovel' tail.

The curious carving is said to be linked to the Bulmer family, who at one time owned the nearby Bull Inn. The hostelry was probably named after the mighty beast known as the Ketton (or Durham) Ox that was bred by the Colling brothers at the nearby hamlets of Ketton and Barmpton.

Carving on the wall in Bull Wynd, near Darlington market place.

POST OFFICE MILE POSTS

MYSTERIOUS MILE MARKERS

Dotted around Darlington's roadways are a handful of metal posts bearing the inscription '1 mile G.P.O.' Ten of these mileposts appear on the 1897 Ordnance Survey map as 'Post', but today less than half this number survive *in situ*.

It is thought that they date from the 1870s or '80s and were probably connected with the delivery of either telegrams or express mail by messenger to any part of the town or rural district, at a charge of *6d* per mile or part of. They may well indicate distances from the former head post office in Northgate, which is now a clothing store. Lettering on the post is taken as referring to the General Post Office, but the first letter resembles a 'C', so that could refer to the Central Post Office.

All in all, these simple metal posts present quite a mystery.

Milepost in Carmel Road South.

HELL'S KETTLES

FANCIFUL TALES OF BOTTOMLESS POOLS

Elements of mystery surround four curious ponds on the north side of the A167, near Croft-on-Tees. Known as Hell's Kettles, they are reported to have been formed on Christmas Day 1179 when the ground rose to a considerable height and remained in that state all day before falling with an enormous crash when darkness fell.

Local folk feared that the end of the world was nigh, and down the years an amount of folklore grew up around the ponds. Suggestions that they were bottomless was dismissed when the deepest was found to be less than 20ft deep, and although numerous suggestions were put forward about their formation, the most popular theory is that this dramatic movement of the earth's crust was caused by a build-up of gases in the magnesium limestone deposits.

Access

A public right of way runs close to Hell's Kettles between the A167 (north of Croft) to the A66 (close to Blackwell).

Hell's Kettles, near Croft-on-Tees.

MEMORIAL TO MARY JANE ALLEN

CELEBRATING THE SKILLS OF THE STAR OF THE SHOW

Access

The memorial to Mary Jane Allen is positioned close to the chapel in Darlington's West Cemetery.

The collection of gravestones, monuments and memorials in cemeteries provides a wealth of detail about a locality and its residents. Inscriptions are often touching, sometimes informative and perhaps revealing, while some are also highly unusual.

A memorial to Mary Jane Allen, who died on 19 February 1874 aged thirty-two, stands close to the chapel in Darlington's West Cemetery. It takes the form of a stallion and was arranged by her husband, Frederick, proprietor of the Excelsior Co.

Mary Jane Allen was the star of the show with her bareback horse-riding routine, and the company's other acts included: Sillo and Elspa, skilful little gymnasts; Miss Ada Isaacs with her jests, songs and dances; Monsieur Fabien, contortionist; and Mr George Ellison, big boot and clog dancer. The memorial has suffered damage in the past and now has shortened legs. It has also been re-attached to the base, and now faces the wrong way, but remains a highly unusual and evocative memorial.

JOSEPH MALABY DENT'S REMARKABLE CAREER

FROM HUMBLE BEGINNINGS TO A WORLDWIDE PRINTING AND PUBLISHING BUSINESS

Access

Joseph Dent's birthplace, now the Britannia Inn, stands on Archer Street (just north of Bondgate).

Darlington has provided any number of eminent personalities in all walks of life, but perhaps one of the least known, Joseph Malaby Dent, rose from humble beginnings in the town to achieve worldwide fame in the business of printing and distribution of books.

The Dent family moved from Dentdale to Darlington, and Joseph, the tenth of eleven children, was born in a small house (now the Britannia Inn) in Archer Street on 30 August 1849. He attended a dame school in Archer Street until the age of four, and the family moved first to High Row and then to a smaller house in Northgate.

Memorial to Mary Jane Allen in Darlington's West Cemetery.

The Britannia, probable birthplace of Joseph Malaby Dent.

Joseph Dent attended a Wesleyan school where his teacher, Mr Blakelock, fostered an interest in literature, and after leaving school he was apprenticed to a local bookbinder and printer. When the business failed, Dent's apprenticeship was incomplete and he did not have the means to set up his own business.

After considering a stage career, Joseph Dent chose to move to London, where he lodged with his brother whilst seeking a bookbinding business where he could complete his apprenticeship. He married at the age of twenty-one and struggled during the next few years to bring up a young family. After purchasing a second-hand plant, Joseph Dent set up his own business.

Financial assistance was provided by a friend named Carter, and the business prospered. His work for the British and Foreign Schools Society from 1902 onwards brought him back to his hometown of Darlington, and he is probably best known for the establishment of the Everyman Library in 1906.

Joseph Malaby Dent died on 9 May 1926, and in the same year a bronze plaque was unveiled at the entrance to George Dent Nursery School in Darlington's Woodlands Road. It marks the Dent family's links with Darlington and the dales.

THE BRICK TRAIN

A RECENT REMINDER OF THE TOWN'S RAILWAY HERITAGE

Darlington's links with the early stages of railway development are well known, but in the late 1990s the town was given another dramatic reminder of those pioneering days.

'The Brick Train' was unveiled at Morton Park on the north side of the A66 Darlington Bypass on 23 June 1997. Commissioned by William Morrison Supermarkets plc and Darlington Borough Council as part of the year of Visual Arts (in 1996) at a cost of £760,000, it is the work of the Scottish artist, David Mach.

A total of 181,754 bricks include six special bat bricks to allow pipistrelle bats to roost inside the layered structure. Bats were introduced in July 1997 by members of the Durham Bat Group. Building work was completed by the Darlington office of Shepherd Construction Ltd in just twenty-eight weeks between November 1996 and May 1997. Local schools prepared time capsules that were positioned inside the structure.

Standing some 30ft in height, the Brick Train is said to have pushed at the boundaries of brick technology with the use of overhanging layers of bricks, and it certainly catches the attention of thousands of motorists who travel along the A66.

Access

Access and the viewing platform are from the car park of the Morton Park Retail Estate via the B6280/A67 East.

'The Brick Train' on the southern edge of Morton Park.

GIANT REDWOODS (*SEQUOIADENDRON GIGANTEUM*)

IMPRESSIVE REMINDER OF A ROYAL MARRIAGE

Access

The trees dwarf surrounding features located close to the memorial clock in South Park.

Parkland close to the clock tower is dominated by giant redwood trees (*Sequoiadendron Giganteum*) that were planted on 11 March 1863 in celebration of the marriage of HRH Albert Edward, Prince of Wales (later Edward VII), to Princess Alexandra of Denmark.

These fine specimens were planted by Col George John Scurfield (1810-1895), the unofficial squire of Hurworth, and Francis Mewburn, the world's first railway solicitor and Chief Bailiff of Darlington, after the official party had been led to South Park by 15th Durham Volunteers.

They now reach a height of 20m, which is rather shorter than the tallest sequoias in the United Kingdom, standing at 45m at Leod Castle, Inverness. However, even these fall well short of the sequoia in California which reached 90m in 2002.

Information board in South Park with details of the giant redwood trees.

Right: *Giant redwood* (Sequoiadendron Giganteum).

Below: *River Skerne, clock tower and giant redwoods.*

FOWLER MONUMENT

A SIMPLE CLUE TO A PIONEERING AGRICULTURIST

Access

The Fowler
Monument
is flanked by
coronation
oaks close to
the tea pavilion
in South Park.

A simple marble plinth in South Park is flanked by coronation oaks at a location overlooking the lake. It has only a brief inscription: 'John Fowler C.E. 1856', and remains something of a mystery.

In fact, Fowler was a notable Victorian civil engineer and in 1856 he invented a steam plough that could turn over a field more quickly than horse-drawn machinery. The link with Darlington was forged when Fowler married a daughter of Joseph Pease.

When he died in 1864, at the age of thirty-eight, his monument was installed in the grounds of Henry Pease's home in the Pierremont district of Darlington. Originally, it had a model of a double-acting, steam-drawn, multi-furrow plough mounted on the base and the whole structure was moved to the park in 1870.

The Fowler Monument in South Park.

Remaining base of the Fowler Monument.

During the 1970s the upper section was destroyed by vandals, leaving just the base to highlight the work of a pioneering Victorian agriculturist.

DRINKING FOUNTAINS

SUPPLYING WATER TO TOWNSFOLK

Joseph Pease made a major contribution to many aspects of life in the Darlington area. Bronze plaques around his statue at the northern end of High Row highlight his contribution to politics, education, railways and the anti-slavery movement.

At a local level, he presented a total of eight cast-iron drinking fountains to the town. Complete with decorative stone canopies, they are set into roadside walls at locations on important roadways close to the centre of the town.

Access

Examples of the fountains are to be seen at the junction of Milbank Road and Woodland Road, as well as in the wall of the former Grange Hotel in Coniscliffe Road.

This page: *Drinking fountains presented to the town of Darlington by Joseph Pease.*

Drinking fountain in Milbank Road.

BULMER'S STONE

FAMILY RELIC OR TOWN CRIER'S PODIUM?

Darlington's original Technical College building on Northgate was opened by the Duke of Devonshire in 1897, and behind roadside railings stands a large glacial boulder known as Bulmer's Stone. It takes its name either from the Bulmer family, who owned adjacent property, or from a town crier, Willie Bulmer, who is said to have stood on the stone to read news items to townsfolk.

The stone may also have been used for beating yarn when Darlington had a flourishing linen industry. Weavers cottages were demolished in 1897 to make way for the Technical College but the stone remains near to its original site.

Access

The stone is positioned between railings and the former college buildings on the west side of North Road (and just north of the original main entrance).

The Bulmer Stone on North Road.

Information panel with details on the Bulmer Stone.

HITCHING STONE

LINK WITH A CAMPAIGNING JOURNALIST

Several notable buildings in central Darlington were completed in the closing decades of the nineteenth century. Edward Pease (1834-1880) provided money to build the library in Crown Street, which opened in 1885 and was extended in 1933. Outside the red-sandstone and pressed-brick building is a small boulder with a metal ring. A former editor of the *Northern Echo*, W.T. Stead, often used it to tether his pony after travelling to his nearby office from the family home at Grainey Hill Cottage, Hummersknott. In 1880, Mr Stead moved to London to become editor of the *Pall Mall Gazette* and was drowned in the *Titanic* disaster of 1912.

Access
The hitching stone is clearly visible beside the library wall on Crown Street.

The Hitching Stone, on Crown Street.

PUMPS AT TEES COTTAGE WORKS

MASTERPIECES OF MECHANICAL ENGINEERING

Access

Features at the pumping station are regularly open to the public with both steam and gas engines in action. The site is on Coniscliffe Road, close to the Baydale Beck Inn.

The buildings of the Tees Cottage pumping station and its successor, the Broken Scar Treatment Works, dominate the skyline on Coniscliffe Road and here, on the one site, is the entire history of pumped water supply.

From 1849 a number of pumps were installed on premises situated south of the road to lift water from the Tees. After settlement, treatment and filtration, the water was delivered into Darlington, but as demand for water increased, further treatment capacity was established to the north of Coniscliffe Road. In 1926, a major expansion of installations was completed, but original machinery was retained as back-up. Modernisation of the treatment plant brought an increase in capacity during 1955, and in 1972 another extension was added to the thirteen million gallon per day plant.

The water to feed the plant continued to be extracted from the Tees adjacent to the site, and the river level was maintained by discharging the required quantities into the Tees from the Northumbria Water Board's reservoirs in Upper Teesdale.

During 1980 original buildings at the Tees Cottage pumping station were threatened with demolition, but in November 1980 a charitable trust was formed to preserve buildings and equipment. Since then members have carried out restoration work on buildings and equipment, including the three pumping systems which were all the height of innovation in their time.

The beam steam engine pumped more than four million gallons per day before being replaced around 1914 by a gas engine. An electric pumping system from 1926 is of equal rarity.

Tees Cottage pumping station on Coniscliffe Road.

Right: *Tees Cottage pumping station.*

Below: *Broken Scar Treatment Works.*

CAMOUFLAGED TELEPHONE MASTS

TREES IN DISGUISE

Access

The trees/
telephone
masts are on
the perimeter
of Blackwell
Grange Golf
Club, adjacent
to Carmel Road
South (A67).

A strip of woodland lines the eastern edge of Blackwell Grange Golf Club, beside the A67 Carmel Road South. For the most part they are fine mature specimens – mainly coniferous – but in recent years they have been joined by two unlikely 'trees'.

Soaring skywards to a considerable height are two mobile telephone masts covered in a camouflage of synthetic green 'branches'. From a distance the trees look realistic and, as if to emphasise their authenticity, birds have recently nested in one of these so-called trees.

Left and opposite:
*Telephone masts
camouflaged as trees
on the perimeter of
Blackwell Grange Golf
Club.*

AN UNORTHODOX MILITARY MONUMENT

SOUTH AFRICAN WAR MEMORIAL

Access

The memorial is positioned on the south side of Stonebridge, and on the north side of St Cuthbert's Church.

Up and down the country many towns and villages have war memorials in a central location. The most prominent memorials are usually devoted to the men and women who lost their lives in the two world wars, and it is easy to overlook other monuments commemorating those who lost their lives in the South African (or Boer) War that lasted from 1899 to the Peace of Vereeniging (signed on 31 May 1902).

Darlington's Boer War memorial was unveiled on 5 August 1905 by Earl Roberts, and it stands in a prominent position close to Stone Bridge and in the shadow of St Cuthbert's Church. The nature of the memorial has created an amount of discussion and has been described as being rather too aggressive. The soldier's stance seems awkward and ungainly and this perhaps results from the fact that he is leading with the wrong foot (as in the case of a southpaw-style boxer).

South African (or Boer) War Memorial on the north side of St Cuthbert's Church.

FRIENDS' QUAKER MEETING HOUSE AND BURIAL GROUND

LINKS WITH THE TOWN'S QUAKER CITIZENS

Quaker families began to settle in Darlington in the 1660s and they soon became prominent in the town's economic development. Woollen and linen industries became increasingly centralised in their hands, and, during a period of late eighteenth-century growth, the population increased from around 3,500 in 1767 to over 4,500 by 1801. Between 1800 and 1850 there was a further phase of dramatic growth as the town's population increased to more than 12,000, and much of this demographic activity resulted from the opening of the Stockton and Darlington Railway in September 1825.

Successive generations of the Pease family continued to play a part in the development of railways throughout the north-east of England, and the influence of Quaker families such as Pease and Backhouse is found in buildings at many locations in the town.

Access

Friends Quaker Meeting House and Burial Ground is located at No. 6 Skinnergate, Darlington.

Friends' Meeting House, Darlington.

Graveyard of the Friends' Meeting House at No. 6 Skinnergate, Darlington.

Properties such as 'Pease House' on the north side of Houndgate and Northgate Lodge are well-known urban landmarks, but a tranquil setting adjacent to Skinnergate provides a fascinating link with the town's dramatic nineteenth-century growth.

Members of prominent Darlington Quaker families such as Pease and Backhouse are buried in the Meeting House Burial Ground close to the town centre that they largely created.

LEPER HOSPITAL IN THE BAYDALE AREA

MYSTERIOUS LOCATION OF AN EARLY BUILDING OF CARE

Access

The Baydale Beck Inn stands alongside the A67 road across the fields from Low Coniscliffe.

For many years, speculation has persisted about a leper hospital based in buildings at Baydale Farm on low-lying land close to the Tees.

However, it is now believed that the farm buildings were given ecclesiastical features purely for effect and that the actual site of the leper hospital was where the Baydale Beck Inn now stands.

Baydale Beck Inn.

Bibliography & References

REDCAR & CLEVELAND

Bainbridge, N., *Saltburn-by-the-Sea: A Pictorial History*, A.A. Sotheran Ltd, 1977

Cockroft, J., *Redcar and Coatham: A History to the End of World War II*, A.A. Sotheran Ltd, 1980

Harrison, B.J.D. and Dixon G., *Guisborough Before 1900*, G. Dixon, 1981

Hope, Revd E., *History of Marske-by-the-Sea*, A.A. Sotheran Ltd, 1975

Sotheran, P., *Memories of Marske*, A.A. Sotheran Ltd, 1976

Sotheran, P., *Redcar in Restrospect*, A.A. Sotheran Ltd, 1975

STOCKTON-ON-TEES

Sowler, T., *A History of the Town and Borough of Stockton-on-Tees*, Teesside Museums and Art Galleries Department, 1972

Stockton-on-Tees Railway Centenary Committee, *The Railway Centenary 1825-1925*, 1925

MIDDLESBROUGH

Middlesbrough's History in Maps, Cleveland and Teeside Local History Society, 1996

Lillie, W. *The History of Midlesbrough: An Illustration of the Evolution of English History*, County Borough of Middlesbrough, 1968

Moorsom, N., *The Birth and Growth of Modern Middlesbrough*, N. Moorsom, 1967

Tomlin, D. *Past Industry along the Tees*, D.M. Tomlin, 1980

Williams, M., *Pottery That Began Middlesbrough*, 1985

HARTLEPOOL
Mears, A.G., *Tales of Our Town*, 1893
Todd, Revd J., *Hartlepool Records*, Oxford University Press, 1953
Wood, R., *Victorian Delights*, Pan, 1999
Wood, R., *West Hartlepool: The Rise and Development of a Victorian new town*, Hartlepool Corporation, 1967

DARLINGTON
Chilton, J.D., *Jottings Over a Lifetime In and Around Darlington*, Talbot Print, 1981
Dean, S.C., and Clough, U.M., *Darlington as It Was*, Hendon Publishing Co. Ltd, 1974
Flynn, G.J. *Darlington In Old Photographs*, Sutton Publishing Ltd, 1989
Woodhouse, R., *Darlington: A Pictorial History*, Phillimore & Co. Ltd, 1998

Other local titles published by The History Press

County Durham Strange but True
ROBERT WOODHOUSE

County Durham Strange but True illustrates and describes people, places and incidents that are unusual, odd or extraordinary. We discover the truth about flamboyant or eccentric characters, curious buildings, strange place names, weird weather, mazes, standing stones and holes in the ground, unusual customs, local folklore and legend, among many other fascinating items. Robert Woodhouse tells an entertaining story - an alternative history of County Durham that will fascinate residents and visitors alike.

978 0 7509 3731 3

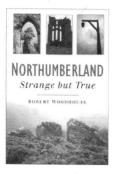

Northumberland Strange but True
JROBERT WOODHOUSE

Robert Woodhouse describes people, places and incidents in Northumberland that are unusual, odd or extraordinary. Containing many little-know facts and richly illustrated with photographs, maps and ingravings, this fascinating collection will entrall anyone interested in the history of the county.

978 0 7509 4067 2

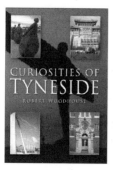

Curiosities of Tyneside
ROBERT WOODHOUSE

Sandwiched between County Durham and Northumberland, Tyneside is one of the most heavily industrialised regions of Britain. This book guides us to over 100 remarkable sights to be found on Tyneside, spanning centuries of history since Roman times.

978 0 7509 4444 1

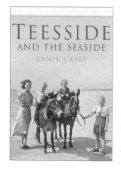

Teesside and the Seaside
ERNIE CRUST

This book is a delightful compilation of more than 220 archive photographs, the majority of which have come from the private collection of a local photographer, the late Jack Wright. It tells the story of Teesside and Redcar seaside from the early 1930s through the war years and finally to the late 1950s. It will captivate those who remember Teesside in days gone by and delight everyone who has ever longed to be beside the seaside.

978 0 7524 4731 5

Visit our website and discover thousands of other History Press books. www.thehistorypress.co.uk

The History Press